my **revisi⏻n** notes

WJEC GCSE
SCIENCE

Jeremy Pollard
Adrian Schmit

HODDER
EDUCATION
AN HACHETTE UK COMP

This material has been endorsed by WJEC and offers high quality support for the delivery of WJEC qualifications. While this material has been through a WJEC quality assurance process, all responsibility for the content remains with the publisher.

The publisher would like to thank the following for permission to reproduce copyright material:

p.25 'Outrage over DNA database' article from http://www.walesonline.co.uk/news/wales-news/2008/01/16/outrage-over-dna-database-91466-20354577/ (January 16 2008) Reproduced by permission of Media Wales Ltd; **p.51** Quotes from New Scientist June 2006.

Past paper exam questions reproduced by permission of WJEC.

Photo credits:
p.8 Eye Ubiquitous/Rex Features; **p.10** © Alonbou – Fotolia.com; **p.33** *both* Becca Law; **p.37** © blickwinkel/Alamy; **p.43** © Alexander Raths – Fotolia; **p.51** © Cristiana Ceppas/Alamy; **p.101** Jane Songhurst – Fotolia.

Although every effort has been made to ensure that website addresses are correct at time of going to press, Hodder Education cannot be held responsible for the content of any website mentioned. It is sometimes possible to find a relocated web page by typing in the address of the home page for a website in the URL window of your browser.

Orders: please contact Bookpoint Ltd, 130 Milton Park, Abingdon, Oxon OX14 4SB. Telephone: (44) 01235 827720. Fax: (44) 01235 400454. Lines are open 9.00–17.00, Monday to Saturday, with a 24-hour message answering service. Visit our website at www.hoddereducation.co.uk

© Adrian Schmit and Jeremy Pollard 2012
First published in 2012 by
Hodder Education
An Hachette UK Company,
338 Euston Road
London NW1 3BH

Impression number   5
Year   2016   2015   2014   2013

Cover photo © PASIEKA/Science Photo Library
Illustrations by Barking Dog Art
Typeset in Cronospro-Lt 12 points by Datapage (India) Pvt. Ltd.
Printed in India
A catalogue record for this title is available from the British Library.
ISBN 978 1 444 17170 9

Get the most from this book

This book will help you revise the contents of the new WJEC GCSE Science specification. You can use the contents list on pages 4 and 5 to plan your revision, topic by topic. Tick each box when you have:

1 revised and understood a topic

2 tested yourself

3 checked your answers online.

You can also keep track of your revision by ticking off each topic heading through the book. You may find it helpful to add your own notes as you work through each topic.

Tick to track your progress

Examiner tips

Throughout the book there are Examiner tips that explain how you can boost your final grade.

Higher tier

Some parts of the WJEC specification are tested only on higher-tier exam papers. These sections are highlighted using a red and yellow strip down the side of the page.

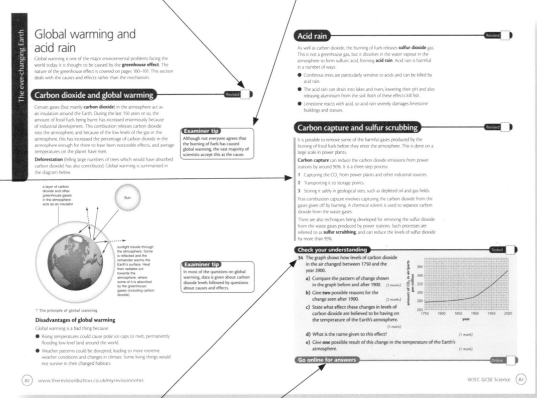

Check your understanding

Use these questions at the end of each section to make sure that you have understood every topic.

Go online

Go online to check your answers at **www.therevisionbutton.co.uk/myrevisionnotes**

Contents and revision planner

P Physics

Variety of life

Variety and classification

Revised

All living things vary in shape, size and complexity. In order to make sense of this, scientists **classify** living things into a series of groups, in each of which the organisms have similar features.

- Plants can be grouped into **flowering** and **non-flowering** types.

- Animals can be grouped into **vertebrates** (with a backbone) and **invertebrates** (without a backbone). The invertebrates are not strictly a classification group, because they share the absence of a feature, rather than having common features.

- Microorganisms are microscopic organisms which can be grouped into **bacteria**, **fungi** and **algae**.

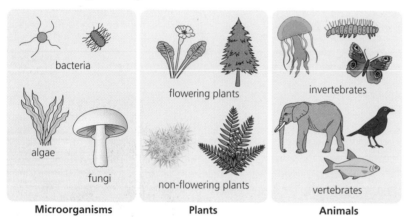

bacteria

algae

fungi

Microorganisms

flowering plants

non-flowering plants

Plants

invertebrates

vertebrates

Animals

- Scientists use **morphological features** (the shape and structure of the body) and the structure of the DNA to group living things.

- Scientists can tell how closely related two organisms are by comparing their **DNA**. DNA is the chemical which makes genes, and the more similar the DNA is, the more closely related the organisms are. This technique is called **DNA hybridisation** or **genetic profiling**. It is a more accurate way of checking how closely related two oraganisms are than just looking for common features.

- Each large group is split into smaller and smaller groups. As the groups get smaller, the organisms are more closely related and share more features.

- Every living organism is given a **scientific name** by an international committee. This avoids confusion when talking about the same organism in different languages. The non-scientific, or common name, is different in different countries.

- Living things used to be classified into **five kingdoms** – bacteria, single-celled organisms, fungi, plants and animals. Recently, classification into **three domains** (ancient bacteria, bacteria and all organisms with a nucleus) has become more popular.

Homo sapiens

Organisms and the environment

In order to survive in their environment, living organisms have to become adapted to the physical conditions, and need to be able to survive alongside other living things. This can affect them in various ways.

● Organisms have structural and behavioural **adaptations** which help them to survive in their environment.

● Organisms have to be able to obtain essential **resources** from their environment. These include food, water and (for plants) light and minerals.

● Some resources may be in limited supply in the environment. Different organisms will have to compete with each other to obtain them. This **competition** will limit their **populations**.

● **Predation** (being eaten by other animals in the environment) can reduce the size of the prey population.

● Population size can also be reduced by **disease** and **pollution**.

> **Examiner tip**
>
> Notice in Question **1** it asks which **feature** (singular). This tells you that for each part only **one** answer is required. If you put two, you may get no marks, even if one is correct.

Check your understanding

1 Read the following information.

● Aye-ayes live on the island of Madagascar.

● They live in trees.

● They have large eyes and large, sensitive ears.

● The aye-ayes listen for insects moving under the bark of trees.

● Their middle finger is very long and pointed.

● Aye-ayes have sharp claws on all their fingers and toes.

● They have a bushy tail that is larger than their body.

Use the information and the drawing to answer the following questions.

Which feature:

a) helps the aye-aye to hunt at night? *(1 mark)*

b) helps the aye-aye find insects under the bark of trees? *(1 mark)*

c) helps the aye-aye get the insects from under the bark of trees? *(1 mark)*

d) helps the aye-aye to climb trees? *(1 mark)*

e) helps the aye-aye to **balance** on a tree branch? *(1 mark)*

↑ The aye-aye

2 The hedgehog's common name is the European hedgehog. Its scientific name is *Erinaceus europaeus*. Why do scientists give animals scientific names? Pick **two** correct statements:

A The same common name is used in different countries.

B The same scientific name is used in different countries.

C Different common names are used in different countries.

D Different scientific names are used in different countries. *(2 marks)*

Go online for answers

Humans and the environment

Balancing needs

There are many reasons to conserve wildlife. Humans like to visit or live in countryside containing a variety of animals and plants. This variety of life also provides humans with food and other resources. However, humans also have needs that can conflict with conservation.

● Humans need **homes** in which to live, and the building of homes destroys parts of the natural environment.

● Humans need to produce **food** on a large scale, which means that the natural environment has to be changed to favour the animals and plants that we eat. Natural habitats can be destroyed by people cutting down trees and creating fields.

The **huge population** of humans on the planet means that large areas of natural habitat have been destroyed. The human population is still rising and so the problem is getting worse.

Intensive farming

Intensive farming is farming that uses methods to get as much yield (from either plants or animals) from as small a space as possible. This can involve the use of **fertilisers**, **pesticides**, **disease control** and **battery methods**. These all have advantages and disadvantages. Some methods of intensive farming are listed at the top of the next page.

↑ **Battery-farmed chickens are kept in very confined spaces**

Method	Advantages	Disadvantages
Fertilisers	Increase the yield of the crop	Can wash out of the soil and pollute rivers and streams
Pesticides	Prevent pests from eating or competing with the crop, so increase the yield	Can destroy non-pest organisms Chemicals may stay in the crop and be eaten by humans
Disease control*	Prevents loss of animals or crops to disease	Antibiotics given to animals may remain in the meat when it is eaten by humans
Battery methods	More animals can be kept in a given space Animals use less energy and so need less food Costs are reduced so the meat can be sold cheaply	The animals' quality of life is very poor

*Diseases can be controlled by genetic modification. This is dealt with in the section 'Genetic engineering' on pages 30–31.

Badger culling and bovine TB
Revised

In recent years, farmers have been pressing to have badgers killed (culled) to reduce the numbers of cattle catching **bovine tuberculosis** (TB). The UK government have been undecided whether to allow this because the scientific evidence is not straightforward.

● Badgers can catch bovine TB and pass it on to cattle.

● Many cattle die each year from TB.

● Culling badgers has been effective in some areas, but is not always successful.

● Sometimes, badgers that survive a cull move out of the area and start an infection elsewhere.

● Other methods (e.g. vaccinating badgers) may be effective at controlling the disease.

● Since much of the evidence available is conflicting, more experiments need to be done to improve the evidence for or against culling.

> **Examiner tip**
> Exam questions often require you to think about a given situation, rather than just remember facts. You do not need to have learnt about the specific scenario (e.g. using systemic pesticides), as you can answer the question by giving it some thought.

Check your understanding
Tested

3 Some hens' eggs are labelled 'free range'. This means that the chickens have been raised with freedom to move around. Eggs that are not free range come from 'battery hens', which have been kept very close together in cages which do not allow them to move around. Many people prefer to buy free range eggs, but they are more expensive.

   a) Assuming no difference in taste, why might people prefer free-range eggs? *(1 mark)*

   b) Suggest **two** reasons why battery eggs are cheaper than free-range eggs. *(2 marks)*

4 Many farmers spray chemical pesticides onto their crops. Some use 'systemic' pesticides which are absorbed into the plant, so that when a pest feeds on the crop it takes in the pesticide.

   a) State **two** advantages of using systemic pesticides, rather than spraying chemicals. *(2 marks)*

   b) Suggest **one** possible disadvantage of using systemic pesticides. *(1 mark)*

Go online for answers
Online

Pollution indicators

Pollution in streams and rivers Revised

Streams and rivers can be polluted in various ways.

- **Sewage** and **fertilisers** used on farm land can be washed through the soil by rainfall and drain into rivers and streams.

- **Chemicals** can leak into rivers that are near factories or industrial sites.

- **Warm water**, which has been used to cool machinery in factories, can also get into rivers. The heat causes increased growth of bacteria.

- Acid rain also runs off land and can pollute fresh water.

- These pollutants can cause:

  - the levels of **oxygen** to fall, killing animals that need a lot of it. **Bacteria** which feed on sewage or dead organisms multiply and use up the available oxygen.

  - the **pH** of the water to change. **Acid rain** and **chemical waste** can lower pH. Many animals and plants can only survive in a narrow range of pH.

  - poisoning. Some chemicals **poison** living organisms. This will also lead to a rise in bacteria feeding on the dead organisms, and so the oxygen levels will again drop.

  - leaching. Acid rain can leach **aluminium** from soil into rivers. Aluminium is poisonous to animals in the water.

Indicator species Revised

Different animal and plant species have different levels of tolerance to pollution. This allows certain species to be used as indicators of the level of pollution.

- Some species need clean air or water and are only found in unpolluted environments.

- Some species have a very high tolerance to pollution and are found in polluted areas.

- These species are often absent from clean areas because they cannot compete with the species that live there. Therefore, if they are found in an area it must be polluted.

- Lichens (an organism which lives on stones and trees) can be killed by sulfur dioxide pollution in the air. Some are more tolerant than others, and so the types of lichen found can be used to assess air pollution.

- Scientists can count the numbers of these different 'indicator species' in an area to get an idea of how polluted it is.

↑ A lichen, *Physcia tenella*, growing on a branch

- Scientists can monitor the **levels of oxygen** in the water to indicate the level of pollution. Lots of bacteria in the water will lower the level of oxygen.

- **Testing pH** gives information on pollution. A variety of factors can change pH but if it varies much from pH 7, organisms are likely to be adversely affected.

- **Mathematical 'models'** can use these measurements to analyse and predict future effects.

> **Examiner tip**
>
> Question **5** part **c)** has two marks available. This means that you need to make two points. You could refer to the level of pollution, but if so, you will need to explain **why** pollution levels altered for the second mark.

Check your understanding

Tested

5 The rat-tailed maggot is an insect larva that can live in polluted water. It is less common in clean water. The graph shows the numbers of rat-tailed maggots found at different points in a stream. There is a farm near the stream, and sewage from the farm sometimes pollutes the stream.

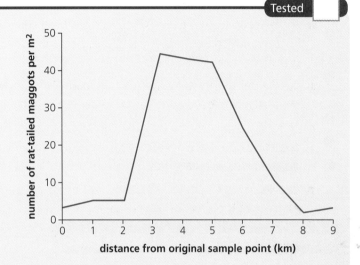

a) How many kilometres from the original sample point would you expect to find the farm? Give a reason for your answer.

(2 marks)

b) Which part of the stream is the most polluted? (1 mark)

c) Suggest a reason for the decline in the numbers of rat-tailed maggots between 5 and 8 km from the original starting point. (2 marks)

6 Read the following information about lichens and air pollution.

- Lichens grow on trees and buildings.

- Scientists use lichens as indicators of air pollution.

- Air polluted with sulfur dioxide gas can kill lichens because sulfur builds up inside them. Some species are more sensitive to air pollution than others.

Form of lichen	Flat	Leafy	Hairy
Level of pollution where lichen is found	Low, medium and high	Medium and low	Low

↑ Lichen indicators

From this information only:

a) Name the gas which pollutes the air. (1 mark)

b) How does this substance kill lichens? (1 mark)

c) Which lichen is best at surviving pollution? (1 mark)

Scientists found much leafy lichen in a woodland but no hairy lichen.

d) What was the level of pollution? (1 mark)

Go online for answers

Online

Types of pollution

Fertilisers and sewage

Streams, rivers and ponds can get polluted when they are close to farmland. Chemical fertilisers and untreated sewage from farm animals can get into the water. This can cause the death of wild animals, due to the following sequence of events.

- Untreated sewage is fed on by bacteria, which use up the oxygen in the water.

- Sewage and fertilisers both stimulate the growth of plants.

- The biggest effect is on algae (microscopic plants), because they grow very fast.

- Algae may completely cover the surface of ponds; this prevents light getting to the plants below the surface, which then die.

- The algae have a short life cycle, so a lot of dead algae accumulate in the water.

- The dead plants and algae provide food for huge numbers of bacteria.

- The bacteria use up the oxygen in the water.

- Some animals living in the water (e.g. fish) need a lot of oxygen and 'suffocate' when the oxygen levels are low.

Examiner tip

Algae covering the surface only applies to ponds. The movement of water in rivers and streams would prevent this.

Heavy metals and pesticides

These pollutants can get into food chains and affect humans. Humans are at the top of food chains, where the effect of the pollutants is at its worst.

- Heavy metals are often present in industrial waste. If this waste gets into fresh water, it will enter the food chain because it will be absorbed by animals and plants in the water.

- Pesticides can be washed into fresh water, but as they are sprayed onto food crops they can also enter the food chain directly.

- The chemicals get more concentrated as they pass through the food chain, because the animals at each stage eat large numbers of the organisms earlier in the chain (see the diagram on page 13). This is called **bioaccumulation**.

- The pollutants can build up to toxic levels in the animals towards the top of the food chain.

- DDT was a popular pesticide in the 1940s to 1960s. Scientific evidence accumulated during that time about its harmful effects on wildlife and possible dangers to human beings. The evidence also showed that DDT remained in the environment for a long time. This led to DDT being banned in the USA in 1972 and in the UK in 1984.

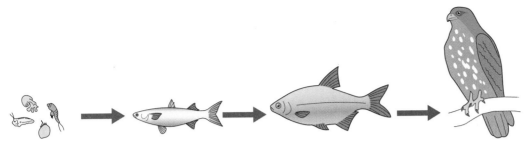

Plankton
Absorb pesticide
Pesticide level – 0.04 ppm

Small fish
Eats lots of plankton
Pesticide level – 0.5 ppm

Large fish
Eats lots of small fish
Pesticide level – 2 ppm

Bird of prey
Eats lots of large fish
Pesticide level – 25 ppm

↑ A food chain: as you move along the food chain the level of pesticide increases

Examiner tip

The chart in Question **7** is complex and the information given in the question is important because it explains features of the graph that will be needed when answering the question. Read the text carefully and make sure you understand it before writing your answers.

Examiner tip

Remember that with Quality of Written Communication questions like Question **8**, the examiners will be looking for clear explanations. If you get the basic facts right but your explanation is not clear or lacks detail, you may lose marks. See pages 110–111 for more help answering QWC questions.

Check your understanding

Tested

7   The data shown in the diagram shows the biomass of organisms and the mass of insecticide found in organisms living in or near a lake. The areas of the rectangles (drawn to scale) represent the total mass of the organisms. The number of dots in each rectangle indicates the mass of insecticide found in the organisms.

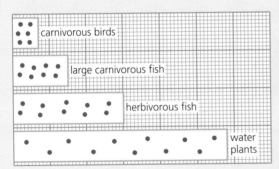

a) Name the organisms in the diagram in which:

   i)   the mass of insecticide is greatest.   *(1 mark)*

   ii) the concentration of insecticide per unit mass is greatest.   *(1 mark)*

b) Use the diagram to estimate the mass of carnivorous fish that could be supported by 1000 kg of herbivorous fish.   *(1 mark)*

c) Describe **two** possible environmental disadvantages of the continuous use of an insecticide near the lake.   *(2 marks)*

8   Fertiliser used on a farm field was washed into a nearby stream.
Some time later, fishermen reported dead fish floating in the stream.
Explain the sequence of events that led to the death of the fish.   *(6 marks QWC)*

Go online for answers

Online

Food chains and food webs

Energy from the Sun

All living organisms get their energy either directly or indirectly from the Sun's radiation. Green plants and algae use the Sun's energy directly via photosynthesis, which makes food for them. Other organisms feed on the plants or algae, and then are eaten by others, as shown below.

Producers (green plants or algae)	A small percentage of the light reaching the producers is converted into food (chemical energy).
eaten by	
First stage consumers (herbivores)	These organisms get their energy by feeding on plants.
eaten by	
Second stage consumers (carnivores)	Most carnivores feed on first stage consumers.
eaten by	
Third stage consumers (carnivores)	Some carnivores feed on second stage consumers, but this is unusual because second stage consumers are often quite large and have smaller populations than herbivores. It is rare for anything to feed on a third stage consumer.

A **food chain** shows the transfer of energy between organisms, symbolised by arrows. Food chains are inter-linked to form **food webs**.

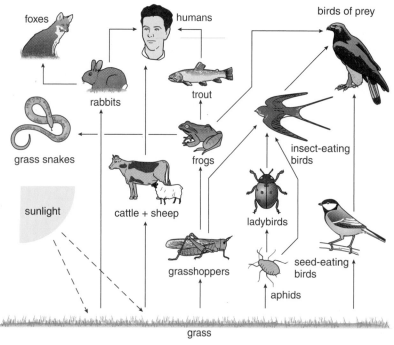

⬆ **A food web. The arrows show the flow of energy**

Energy loss in food chains

Most of the energy from the Sun's radiation never enters food chains. It may 'miss' plants and, even if it does shine on them, photosynthesis can only convert a small percentage of it into food.

The food that a plant makes is not all available to animals, and energy is lost at each stage in a food chain.

- Whenever any organism **respires** (to get the energy from its food) some energy is lost as **heat**.
- All organisms use energy to **maintain** and **repair** their cells.
- Although the organisms may use energy to grow, this is not wasted, as it provides more for a predator to eat.
- Animals also use energy for **movement**, and mammals and birds also use it to **maintain their body temperature**.
- Herbivores rarely eat the whole of a plant (roots and shoots).
- Carnivores often do not eat the whole animal (e.g. bones).
- Animals cannot usually digest every part of the food they eat, so there is unused energy in their faeces.

The loss of energy at each stage means that food chains usually cannot 'last' for more than four or five stages. It also means that the populations get smaller as you go along the chain.

Examiner tip

Question **9** part **a)** is a typical exam question on this topic. You don't get marks for saying the arrows show 'what eats what'. You have to name a process. Look in the text on these pages for the best answer.

Examiner tip

Question **9** part **c)** ii) says pick the correct answer. That (and the fact that there is only one mark) tells you that there is only **one** correct answer. If you put two down, you will lose the mark, even if one is correct.

Check your understanding

Tested

9 The diagram shows a food chain. Answer the following questions using the diagram.

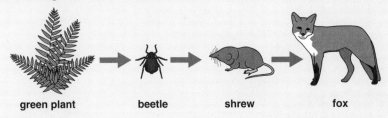

green plant → beetle → shrew → fox

a) What do the arrows in the food chain show? *(1 mark)*

b) i) Name the producer and state its source of energy. *(2 marks)*

ii) Name **one** carnivore in the chain. Give a reason for your choice. *(2 marks)*

c) i) State **one** way in which energy is lost from a food chain. *(1 mark)*

ii) Megan counted the number of these animals in a habitat. What would be the result? Pick the correct answer:

  A More foxes than shrews

  B Fewer beetles than shrews

  C More beetles than shrews *(1 mark)*

10 Look at the diagram of the food web on page 14. The population of frogs has decreased significantly in recent years. What affect might this have on the following populations? Give reasons for your answers.

a) Grass snakes. *(2 marks)*

b) Grasshoppers. *(2 marks)*

c) Insect eating birds. *(2 marks)*

Go online for answers

Online

WJEC GCSE Science

Ecological pyramids

Constructing pyramids

Revised

Food chains show the feeding relationships between organisms in an environment, but they give no indication of the population sizes of the organisms at the different stages. This can be done by constructing an **ecological pyramid**. These can be pyramids of **number**, which record the numbers in each stage, or pyramids of **biomass**, which record the total mass of the population at each stage of the food chain. This is shown in the diagram below.

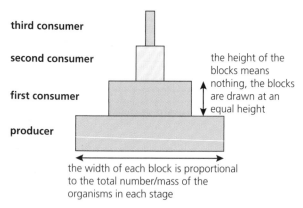

third consumer

second consumer

the height of the blocks means nothing, the blocks are drawn at an equal height

first consumer

producer

the width of each block is proportional to the total number/mass of the organisms in each stage

↑ The ecological pyramid

These diagrams should be pyramid shaped, because there has to be enough food at any level to provide for the next level up. Each first consumer would normally need to eat a large number of producers to survive, and each second consumer would need to eat a large number of first consumers, and so on.

Examiner tip

Questions on ecological pyramids nearly always involve drawing a pyramid from information supplied, or interpreting pyramids. You should ensure that you can do both of these things.

Pyramids of number and biomass

Revised

Pyramids of number are occasionally the 'wrong shape'. This happens if organisms in an earlier stage are much **larger** than those at the next stage. This is shown in the diagram on page 17.

The usual situations where this happens are:

● when the producer is a tree. The tree is much larger than the animals which feed on it, so one tree can feed a much larger number of primary consumers.

● when a consumer is a parasite (e.g. fleas living on dogs). As the dog is much larger than the fleas, hundreds of fleas can live on one dog. In this case the flea will be a third stage consumer, and that block will be very wide.

Pyramids of biomass are almost always pyramid shaped, because they are drawn using the mass of the organisms, and so that takes account of size. For example, although one tree could feed thousands of insects, the total mass of the tree would be much greater than the total mass of all of those insects.

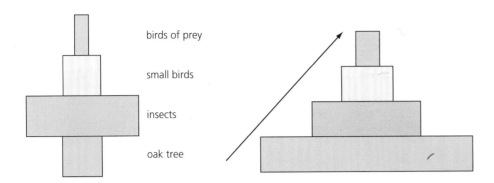

birds of prey

small birds

insects

oak tree

↑ a) A pyramid of numbers for a woodland ecosystem and b) a pyramid of biomass for the same ecosystem

Examiner tip

Notice that in question **11** part **c)** the words **to scale** are in bold. When anything is put in bold it means it is an important instruction to follow, if you are to get full marks for the question.

Check your understanding   Tested

11 The following food chain was found in a garden.

lettuce ⟶ greenfly ⟶ ladybird ⟶ blue tit

a) Name the producer in this food chain.   (1 mark)

The following data was collected on this food chain.

Organism	Number in the food chain	Mass of each organism (g)	Total biomass of organisms (g)
lettuce	6	15	90
greenfly	300	0.1	
ladybird	28	0.5	
blue tit	1	8	

b) Complete the table by calculating the total biomass for each of the organisms in the food chain. One has been done for you.   (1 mark)

c) Give **one** way in which energy is lost from this food chain.   (1 mark)

12 Three food chains are shown below:

A cabbage ⟶ snail ⟶ thrush ⟶ cat

B oak tree ⟶ woodlouse ⟶ shrew ⟶ fox

C lettuce ⟶ slug ⟶ hedgehog ⟶ flea

a) Match the three pyramids of number below to the correct food chain (A, B or C).   (3 marks)

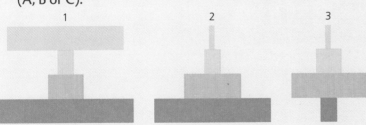

1   2   3

b) Sketch what pyramid 3 would look like if it was drawn as a pyramid of biomass instead of a pyramid of number. Explain the difference.   (2 marks)

Go online for answers   Online

Decay and the carbon cycle

Decay and its importance

Revised

Decay is the breakdown of material through the action of microorganisms – **bacteria** and **fungi**. The material decayed may be waste materials from organisms, the dead bodies of plants and animals, or materials from living organisms which humans use for food.

Decay is a good thing for the following reasons:

● Waste materials and dead bodies are **broken down**, and so do not build up in the environment.

● The **nutrients** in the waste material and dead bodies are **released** back into the environment. If decay in the environment is prevented, then important chemicals can be locked into the dead material. This happened with the formation of fossil fuels, which were formed in conditions which prevented decay. The carbon locked in the fossil fuels was only released again when humans started burning those fuels.

Decay can be inconvenient for the following reasons:

● The microorganisms use up **oxygen** and produce **carbon dioxide**, because they respire. This can sometimes deprive other organisms of the oxygen they need.

● Decay of food is a nuisance to humans.

Useful materials that are released by decay (for example carbon, nitrogen and phosphorus) can be taken up by other organisms. This results in nutrient cycles. In a stable community, the processes which remove materials are balanced by others which return materials.

The carbon cycle

Revised

Life is carbon-based and there is a fixed supply of carbon on the planet. For life to survive, it is essential that this carbon is recycled. This is done by the carbon cycle.

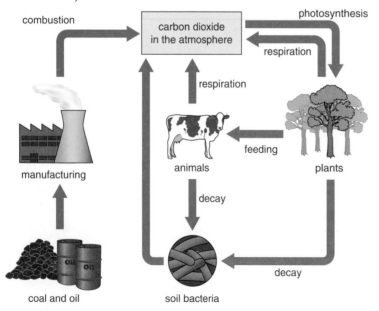

↑ The carbon cycle

The carbon cycle depends on these processes:

- **Photosynthesis**, in which green plants extract carbon dioxide from the air and convert it into glucose.
- **Respiration**, which releases the carbon dioxide back into the air.
- **Feeding**, which is the way in which the carbon gets from plants to animals.
- **Death**, which provides materials for microorganisms to feed on.
- **Decay**, which involves respiration by bacteria and fungi.

In addition to the natural carbon cycle, burning fossil fuels releases large quantities of carbon dioxide back into the atmosphere.

Examiner tip

There are some really easy marks available in Question **13** part **a)**. The answers to all parts of the question can be found in the information given. Look out for easy marks like these in the early questions in the exam paper.

Check your understanding   Tested ☐

13 Garden waste such as leaves, grass and twigs can be piled into a heap called a compost heap.

   Microbes break down the waste material while they feed on it. They respire aerobically, so the heap must be mixed regularly to add air. The decayed material forms compost, which is spread on the garden to improve the soil.

   a) From this information:

   i)   Give **two** examples of plant material which can decay in a compost heap.   *(2 marks)*

   ii) Give the name for decayed plant waste.   *(1 mark)*

   iii) Why is the decayed plant waste spread on the garden?   *(1 mark)*

   b) i) Name **one** type of microbe that causes decay.   *(1 mark)*

   ii) Name the gas which microbes need for respiration.   *(1 mark)*

14 The diagram below shows an outline of the carbon cycle.

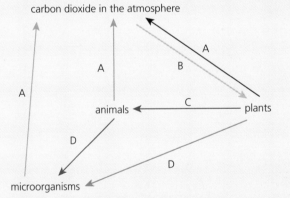

   a) Name the processes A, B, C and D in the diagram.   *(4 marks)*

   b) State **one** other way, not shown in the diagram, that carbon dioxide is released into the atmosphere.   *(1 mark)*

Go online for answers   Online ☐

The nitrogen cycle

The importance of nitrogen

Revised ☐

Nitrogen is a vital element for all living things. It is needed to make **proteins**, which are themselves needed as raw material for the building of new cells and the repair of old ones. Whenever an organism is growing, it needs a lot of protein and so there is a demand for nitrogen. Plants can make carbohydrates by photosynthesis, and these are easily converted into fats, but for proteins the plants need nitrogen. This is absorbed as nitrates from the soil. Plants cannot use gaseous nitrogen, which is the commonest gas in our atmosphere. Only certain bacteria can use nitrogen gas, converting it into nitrates, which the plants absorb.

The nitrogen cycle

Revised ☐

There is a limited supply of nitrogen on the Earth, and so for life to be sustained it has to be recycled. The nitrogen cycle is shown below:

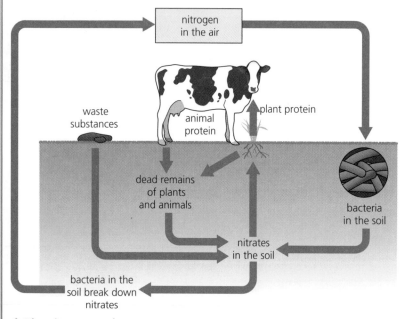

⬆ **The nitrogen cycle**

- The cycle is dependent on the activity of various bacteria.
- Bacteria use nitrogen from the air and convert it into nitrates, which plants can absorb and use.
- Animals get their nitrogen by eating plant proteins.
- Animal waste returns nitrogen to the soil. Urea contains a lot of nitrogen, but some is also present in faeces.
- Nitrogen is also returned to the soil when animals and plants die, and their bodies are broken down by **decomposers** (bacteria and fungi).
- Body proteins and urea are converted into ammonia during decomposition.

- Soil bacteria can change this ammonia into nitrates, which can then be re-used by plants.

- Another type of bacteria changes soil nitrates back into gaseous nitrogen, which is released back into the atmosphere to complete the cycle.

Urea and urease

Revised

The bacteria which break down urea do so using the enzyme **urease**.

urea $\xrightarrow{\text{urease}}$ ammonia + carbon dioxide

As an enzyme-catalysed reaction, it is influenced by various factors.

- Warm temperatures speed up the action of the enzyme, but if the temperature increases above about 60 °C, the enzyme is destroyed (**denatured**) and the reaction stops.

- The optimum pH for urease is about 7. If the pH gets much higher or lower than 7, the enzyme will denature.

- Increasing the concentration of the urease or urea can speed up the reaction, as long as the other factors allow it.

Examiner tip

Remember that with Quality of Written Communication questions like Question **16**, the examiners will be looking for clear explanations. If you get the basic facts right but your explanation is not clear or lacks detail, you may lose marks. See pages 110–111 for more help answering QWC questions.

Check your understanding

Tested

15 The flow diagram shows part of the nitrogen cycle in a field grazed by cows.

   a) Name the processes M, N and K.　　　*(3 marks)*

   b) Name the chemical L and the enzyme X.　　*(2 marks)*

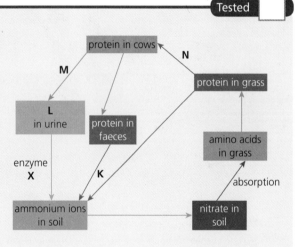

16 Bethan has a grassy field at the back of her house. She noticed that the grass was much longer at certain places in the field. She found clover growing amongst the grass in all of these places. Clover roots have structures called root nodules, which contain bacteria that convert nitrogen into nitrates. Suggest a reason for the grass growing much longer near clover.　*(6 marks QWC)*

17 Sarah and Richard did an experiment to investigate the effect of increasing urease concentration on the rate of breakdown of urea. They measured the volume of carbon dioxide gas given off in 5 minutes. They controlled the pH at 7 and the temperature at 40 °C. Their results are shown in the table:

   a) Suggest an explanation for these results.　　*(1 mark)*

   b) Why did Sarah and Richard keep the reaction at 40 °C rather than at room temperature?　*(1 mark)*

Concentration of urease (%)	Volume of gas given off in 5 minutes (cm³)
1	12
2	11
3	12
4	13
5	11

Go online for answers

Online

Chromosomes, genes and DNA

Definitions

- **Genes** are found in the cell nucleus and determine all the inherited characteristics of an organism.
- Genes are linked together in long strings that are called **chromosomes**.
- **DNA** is the chemical molecule that makes up the genes.

The way in which DNA, genes and chromosomes are interrelated is shown in the diagram.

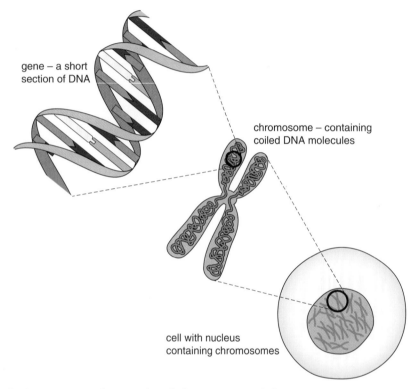

gene – a short section of DNA

chromosome – containing coiled DNA molecules

cell with nucleus containing chromosomes

↑ **The structure of a gene in relation to DNA and chromosomes**

More about genes and chromosomes

The full set of chromosomes found in a body cell consists of pairs of chromosomes. One of each pair originally came from the male parent in the sperm or pollen, and the other came from the female parent in the egg cell. In humans, for instance, there are 46 chromosomes, 23 of which came from the mother and 23 from the father.

This means that genes also occur in pairs, because the pairs of chromosomes contain the same genes as each other. These pairs of genes both control the same feature but they are not necessarily identical, because genes come in different forms, called **alleles**. For example, the human ear lobe gene can be either a 'lobe present' allele or a 'lobe absent' allele, and the gene which decides your blood group has three alleles – A, B and O.

> **Examiner tip**
>
> Exam candidates often get confused by the difference between a gene and an allele. Make sure you know the difference, and can explain it clearly.

DNA is a very unusual molecule because it can make copies of itself. When a cell divides, the DNA duplicates itself so that each of the two new cells can receive a full set of genes. DNA contains coded information for the production of different types of protein. The proteins a cell makes determine how the cell functions, and this is how genes in the DNA control the characteristics of the organism.

Examiner tip

Question **19** part **a)** is really just a puzzle, and you do not need to recall any biology to get the marks. In almost every paper there are some marks for problem-solving exercises like this. Don't be put off by not 'remembering' the answer.

Check your understanding ─────────────────── Tested

18 Fill in the gaps in the following passage about cells.

The characteristics of living organisms are controlled by structures called _____, which are found in long chains called _____ inside the cell's _____. These structures are made of a chemical called_____, which contains a code which controls the manufacture of _____ by the cell.

(5 marks)

19 DNA contains a code which arranges amino acids in an order to form proteins. The code is represented by the letters A, G, T and C. This simplified diagram shows a strand of DNA with its code and amino acids being arranged to form a protein.

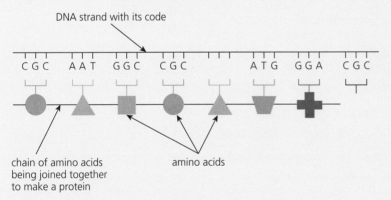

DNA strand with its code

C G C   A A T   G G C   C G C   A T G   G G A   C G C

chain of amino acids being joined together to make a protein

amino acids

a) Complete the diagram by:

i) drawing the missing amino acid (1 mark)

ii) writing in the missing piece of the code. (1 mark)

b) A mutation occurred which changed the code in the strand of DNA shown above. Suggest what effect this would have on the protein which is formed. (1 mark)

20 **a)** Explain the difference between the following:

i) a gene and an allele. (1 mark)

ii) a chromosome and a nucleus. (1 mark)

b) Which of the following is the **best** description of the function of DNA? (1 mark)

A DNA is a chemical which controls the proteins made by the cell.

B DNA is found in the cell's nucleus.

C DNA can be extracted from a cell and analysed.

D DNA is what genes are made from.

Go online for answers ─────────────────── Online

DNA analysis

Overview

DNA is the chemical which makes up the genes of all living organisms. Apart from **identical twins** and **clones**, all organisms have a unique set of genes, and so their DNA is different from all other living things. These differences are quite small, as the DNA of living things also has many common features.

It is now possible for scientists to analyse tiny samples of DNA. The techniques used are **DNA profiling**, which is mainly used for identification, and **DNA sequencing**, which is used to find out about an individual's genes.

DNA profiling

DNA profiling is a way of analysing a DNA sample. It is also known as **genetic profiling**. The DNA is split into short sections which are then analysed, separating the chemicals in the DNA into a series of 'bands' on a gel. The pattern of the bands gives a 'genetic profile'. Everyone's DNA is different (apart from identical twins) and the profile can be used to identify a person with near certainty (the chances of two people who are not identical twins having the same profile is about a billion to one). The amount of DNA needed for testing is incredibly small, and even a few cells provide enough DNA to test. The uses for DNA profiling are:

> **Examiner tip**
>
> Genetic profiling is often referred to as genetic fingerprinting. This term is not a scientific term and will not be accepted as an answer in exams.

- **Investigating crime**. Criminals nearly always leave some DNA at the scene of a crime. This DNA can then be compared to that of suspects.

- **Paternity testing**. A person's DNA profile will be different from their parents', but it will show many similarities. These can be used to decide who the natural father of a child is, when it is disputed.

- **Identification of victims**. DNA profiling has been used to help identify the victims of the 9/11 bombing in New York, and unknown soldiers killed in World War I, by comparing DNA with possible living relatives.

- Discovering the presence of a gene which may cause a **genetic disorder** or **disease**.

- **Comparing the DNA of different organisms** to discover how closely related they are. Closely related organisms will have DNA base sequences that are very similar to one another. The closer the relationship, the more similar the DNA will be.

Some people have objections to certain aspects of DNA analysis.

- During police investigations, DNA samples of innocent people may be taken and kept on record for a time. Some people believe this is an infringement of their civil liberties.

- DNA sequencing may discover a disorder which is not yet obvious, or the likelihood of some future health problem. If this information was discovered by employers or insurance companies, it may affect that person's career, or the cost of their health or life insurance.

- It may be found that a person is more likely than average to suffer from a particular condition in the future. This is a statistical probability, not a certainty, and it could cause the person stress which later turns out to have been unnecessary.

Examiner tip

When questions use the word **suggest** it always means that there is more than one acceptable answer.

Check your understanding   Tested

21 The following front page article appeared in the Western Mail newspaper in January 2008.

> **Outrage as one in ten of us is on the DNA database**
>
> Almost one in ten people in Wales is on the national DNA database. Many of the 264,420 people on the database have never been charged with any criminal offence but their DNA sample is kept for life.

a) Suggest **one** reason why some people, who have never been charged with an offence, object to their DNA samples being kept on record.   *(1 mark)*

b) Suggest **one** advantage of the police keeping a DNA database.   *(1 mark)*

22 Below are some DNA profiles. Sample A was taken from the scene of a crime. The other samples are from four people who police suspect of committing the crime.

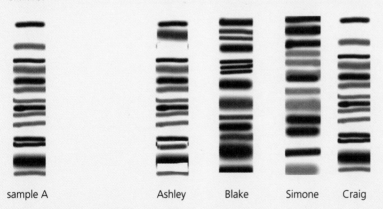

sample A   Ashley   Blake   Simone   Craig

a) On the basis of the samples, who do you think is the criminal? Give a reason for your answer.   *(2 marks)*

b) Two of the suspects are related. Who do you think the related suspects are? Explain your answer.   *(3 marks)*

c) Explain why genetic profiling can provide evidence in more cases than normal fingerprinting can.   *(2 marks)*

Go online for answers   Online

Gamete formation

A different type of cell division

Normally, when cells divide, the new 'daughter' cells receive a full set of chromosomes, so that they can function. When **gametes** (sex cells) are formed, though, this would cause problems. Two gametes fuse during fertilisation to make just one new cell. If the gametes had a full set of chromosomes, then the new cell would have twice as many chromosomes as it should.

To get around this, gametes are formed by a special type of cell division that only passes on a **half set of chromosomes**. Remember the chromosomes are paired, and during gamete formation **one of each pair** of chromosomes is passed on.

In normal cell division, all the new cells are genetically identical, but that's not the case with gametes. The half sets of chromosomes they receive will be different combinations, so the gametes are **not genetically identical**.

When fertilisation occurs, the gametes fuse together and the new cell once again has the normal number of chromosomes. The diagram below summarises what happens in humans.

> **Examiner tip**
>
> This process is called 'meiosis'. Meiosis is a biological term that the specification says you do not have to know. Any term that is not in the specification will be defined in the question. If it *is* in the specification though, you are expected to know it.

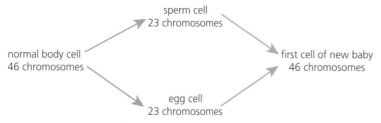

⬆ **How the number of chromosomes changes before, during and after fertilisation**

Sex determination

One particular pair of chromosomes decides whether a baby will be a boy or a girl. These are called the **sex chromosomes**. In girls, the pair of chromosomes look the same. Both are x-shaped, and they are called X chromosomes. In boys, the two chromosomes look different – one is x-shaped, but the other looks more like a Y. We say that girls are 'XX' and boys are 'XY'. The sex of a baby is decided as follows:

- The egg and sperm cells will contain only one of the pair of sex chromosomes.
- All of the egg cells will contain an X chromosome (because that's all females have).
- Half of the sperm cells will contain an X chromosome, the other half will contain a Y chromosome.
- If a sperm containing an X chromosome fertilises the egg, the baby will be XX (a girl).
- If a sperm containing a Y chromosome fertilises the egg, the baby will be XY (a boy).
- This gives an equal probability (50:50) of parents having a boy or a girl.

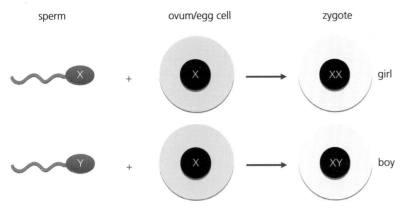

sperm   ovum/egg cell   zygote

↑ How boys and girls are formed during fertilisation

Examiner tip

Remember that with Quality of Written Communication questions like Question **24** part **a)**, the examiners will be looking for clear explanations. If you get the basic facts right but your explanation is not clear or lacks detail, you may lose marks. See pages 110–111 for more help answering QWC questions.

Check your understanding
Tested

23 The diagram shows the production of human gametes (sex cells) by a type of cell division called meiosis. Human body cells have 46 chromosomes.

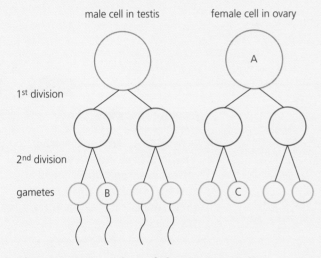

male cell in testis   female cell in ovary

1st division

2nd division

gametes

a) State the number of chromosomes in:

    i) cell A   *(1 mark)*

    ii) cell B.   *(1 mark)*

b) Name the type of gamete labelled C.   *(1 mark)*

c) State **one** reason why meiosis takes place when gametes are produced.   *(1 mark)*

24 a) It is sometimes said that 'The father determines the sex of the baby'. Explain the science behind this statement, in terms of gamete formation.   *(6 marks QWC)*

    b) In 2008, the Office for National Statistics reported that for every 1000 girl babies born, there were 1050 boy babies.

       i) Explain why roughly equal numbers of boy and girl babies are born.   *(3 marks)*

       ii) Suggest a possible reason for the slightly higher number of boys.   *(1 mark)*

Go online for answers
Online

Mendel and inheritance

Gregor Mendel

Gregor Mendel proposed the mechanism of inheritance which gave rise to the science of genetics. His main discoveries were as follows:

● Each characteristic is controlled by a **pair of 'factors'**. We now call these factors alleles.

● If the alleles are the same, e.g. 'tall', then that characteristic is shown by the plant.

● If the alleles are different, e.g. 'tall' and 'dwarf', then the plant shows the characteristic of the **dominant** allele (tall in this case). There is no 'blending' of characteristics of the two alleles.

● The gametes carry just one of the two alleles.

Mendel's work was published, but in a little-read journal, so that it was many years until the scientific community recognised and validated his discoveries. The later discovery of genes and DNA also helped to explain his findings.

Genetic terms

Term	Definition
Genotype	The genetic make-up of an individual, i.e. which alleles it has
Phenotype	The way the gene is seen or expressed, e.g. red flowers, blood group A
Dominant	The character which shows in the heterozygote (see below)
Recessive	The character which is masked in the heterozygote (see below)
F1 and F2	The first (F1) and second (F2) generations in a genetic cross
Selfing	Self-fertilisation
Heterozygous	An individual that has two different alleles of a particular gene
Heterozygote	A heterozygous individual
Homozygous	An individual that has two identical alleles of a particular gene
Homozygote	A homozygous individual

Examiner tip

Genetic terms are used in exam questions. Even if you are not asked what they mean, you will need to know in order to answer the questions, so it is really important that you learn them.

When writing genotypes, the upper case (capital letter) is used for the dominant allele, and the lower case is used for the recessive. The letter chosen is usually the first letter of the dominant character, for example if red flowers are dominant to white, the red allele is given the symbol R, and the white allele is r (not w).

Genetics problems

You can predict the genotypes and phenotypes that result from a particular cross using a Punnett square. The technique is best shown with an example.

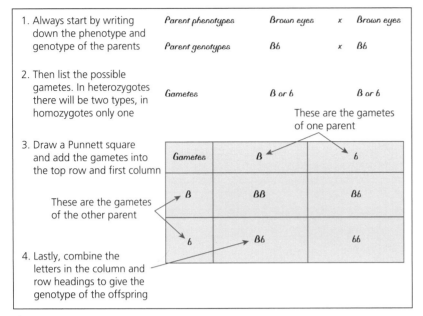

1. Always start by writing down the phenotype and genotype of the parents

| Parent phenotypes | Brown eyes | x | Brown eyes |
| Parent genotypes | Bb | x | Bb |

2. Then list the possible gametes. In heterozygotes there will be two types, in homozygotes only one

| Gametes | B or b | | B or b |

These are the gametes of one parent

3. Draw a Punnett square and add the gametes into the top row and first column

These are the gametes of the other parent

Gametes	B	b
B	BB	Bb
b	Bb	bb

4. Lastly, combine the letters in the column and row headings to give the genotype of the offspring

↑ **How to use a Punnett square**

BB and Bb = brown eyes; bb = blue eyes. There is a 3:1 ratio of brown-eyed children to blue-eyed. The parents are three times more likely to have a brown-eyed child than a blue-eyed one. It does **not** mean that if they have four children, three will have brown eyes and one will be blue-eyed.

Ratios you need to know:

● Aa x Aa gives 3 dominant:1 recessive phenotypes.

● Aa x aa gives 1 dominant:1 recessive.

● AA x aa gives all dominant.

These genetic crosses are used when a characteristic is controlled by just one gene. In humans, most characteristics are controlled by a combination of several genes.

Check your understanding   Tested ☐

When Mendel crossed purple-flowered pea plants with white-flowered pea plants all the offspring (F1) were purple-flowered.

25 **a)** Using the letters R and r to represent the alleles, what would be the genotypes of the purple-flowered parent and the white-flowered parent?   *(2 marks)*

    b) Complete a Punnett square to show the cross between the purple and white-flowered plants.   *(2 marks)*

26 Construct a Punnett square to show how two pea plants when crossed together could produce 50 % purple-flowered and 50 % white-flowered plants.   *(2 marks)*

27 Mendel carried out his experiments on inheritance in the mid 1800s but the importance of his work was not recognised or understood for another 70 years. From the list below choose the statement that best describes the reason for this.

    A Mendel didn't publish his work.

    B DNA and genes hadn't been discovered.

    C Mendel's experiments were badly designed.   *(1 mark)*

Go online for answers   Online ☐

Genetic engineering

Overview

Genetic engineering (also called genetic modification) is the transfer of genes from one species to another. The new gene is incorporated into the DNA of the host organism, and the host then produces the proteins coded for by the new gene. An example of this is in the soya bean plant.

Genetically modified soya beans

- Certain plants are genetically resistant to herbicides.
- The natural soya bean plant is not resistant.
- The herbicide-resistance gene has been identified and transferred to the soya bean plant.
- The soya bean plant then becomes resistant to the herbicide.
- Farmers can spray the herbicide onto their fields, knowing that any weeds will be destroyed, but the soya bean plants will not be affected. This will increase the yield of soya beans.
- Soya beans that are used to produce food for humans will contain this 'unnatural' gene, and some people worry that this may have unforeseen side-effects.

Advantages and disadvantages of GM crops

Plants that have been genetically modified are called **GM crops**. In the UK, there has been public resistance to growing and selling GM crops.

GM crops have certain advantages:

- Crops could be created that are hardy and able to grow in the harsh conditions present in many developing countries.
- Some crops can provide 'biofuels'. These energy-producing crops could save natural resources and so conserve the environment.
- Disease-resistant crops could increase yield.

There are also certain disadvantages:

- Genes introduced into a plant may have unforeseen side-effects when eaten by humans.
- GM crops could spread outside farms and become weeds, which could be difficult to kill.
- If a single company produces a particular GM crop, it would have complete control over the price.

> **Examiner tip**
>
> You do not have to know these specific advantages and disadvantages. Any reasonable suggestion will be credited in the exam.

The need for scientific research

Revised

It is difficult for people and governments to make their minds up about GM crops because there is not enough scientific information available. There is potential for increased yields, but GM crops that have been grown so far don't seem to have much greater yields than the original plants. People are worried about possible side-effects for humans but GM crops that have been made available so far have not caused humans any harm.

It is important for scientists to get more data, and it is important that the data collected is:

● repeatable and reproducible

● based on a large sample

● unbiased.

With more scientific evidence, governments can make sensible policy decisions about GM crops and shoppers will be better informed to make a choice about whether to buy GM foods.

Check your understanding

Tested

28 a) Explain the meaning of the term 'genetic modification (GM)'. *(1 mark)*

b) Give **one** example of a genetic modification that is carried out on a crop plant and state the advantage of the modification. *(2 marks)*

c) Suggest **one** scientific reason why some people are concerned about the genetic modification of plants and animals. *(1 mark)*

29 Genes can be transferred artificially from one organism to another. Scientists transferred a gene, which controls the production of fish oil (such as cod liver oil) from a fish, and a herbicide resistant 'marker' gene into a rapeseed plant. The rapeseed plant will now produce fish oil. The diagram below shows this process.

STAGE 1

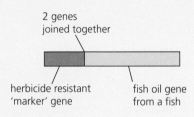

2 genes joined together

herbicide resistant 'marker' gene

fish oil gene from a fish

STAGE 2
new genes are placed into the rapeseed DNA

new genes

rapeseed DNA

STAGE 3
the rapeseed plant should now contain the new genes

a) The scientists don't know whether the gene for the production of fish oil has been successfully introduced into the DNA of the rapeseed plant. Suggest how the herbicide resistant 'marker' gene will allow them to find out. *(1 mark)*

b) Fish oils are said to be good for the heart and nervous system. The world market for fish oils has grown very quickly over the last 25 years. Suggest **one** advantage of growing genetically modified (GM) rapeseed crops for the production of fish oils. *(1 mark)*

c) Suggest why some people are concerned about the transfer of genes from one species to another, especially between animals and plants. *(1 mark)*

Go online for answers

Online

Variation

What is variation? Revised

Individuals of a particular species are different in various ways from all the others in that species. All species therefore show **variation**. These variations may be due to **genetic** or **environmental** causes.

- Examples of genetic variation are: eye colour, hair colour, flower colour, presence of free ear lobes, etc.
- Examples of environmental variation are: scars, piercings, hair style, stunted growth in plants, etc.
- Many of the variations between living things are not visible. For example, there may be differences in the enzymes found inside some of the cells. This may affect the health or fitness of the organism.

Continuous and discontinuous variation Revised

Variation can be classified as continuous or discontinuous.

- In **continuous variation** the individual can be at any point along a range of variation, for example height, where any height is possible between that of the shortest and tallest people in the world.
- In **discontinuous variation** there are distinct categories of variation, for example blood groups, which are A, B, AB and O, without any intermediates.

Variation and reproduction Revised

Sexual reproduction gives rise to offspring which are **genetically different** from their parents, because they contain a mixture of genes from both parents. In asexual reproduction there is only one parent, and so the offspring are all **genetically identical**. These offspring are called **clones**.

Sexual reproduction therefore gives rise to increased variation. This is a good thing for the species. When there is more variety, there is a higher chance that, if the environment changes, there will be a variety that will be able to cope with the change and survive in the new conditions. This helps to ensure the survival of the species over a long period of time.

Mutations Revised

Over the course of evolution, new variations in a species have appeared. These variations are due to 'new' genes that have never been present in the population before.

New genes appear by the process of **mutation**. The DNA of an existing gene becomes changed by mutation. The effect of a mutation depends upon how large it is and whether it occurs in an important area of the DNA. Mutations happen all the time in all organisms, and most mutations have no noticeable effect at all. Many are harmful, but some can be beneficial.

Mutations that happen in the cells of a developing embryo can have particularly large effects, as the mutated cell will go on to form millions of new cells. Some harmful mutations cause conditions which can then be passed on through future generations.

Mutations happen randomly, but the rate of mutation is increased by exposure to ionising radiation.

That is why hospitals try to avoid X-raying pregnant women, because a mutation in an embryo cell could have major effects, as that cell will grow and divide to form many millions of mutated cells in the fully-formed body.

Examiner tip

When a question asks you to show your working, it often means that you will lose marks if you don't. So, even if the working seems obvious and simple, show it when asked.

Check your understanding
Tested

30 There are two types of ear lobe in humans, as shown below.

Students investigated variation in humans. They asked six people how tall they were. They then looked at their ears to see if they had free or attached ear lobes. All the participants were 25-year-old women. The results are shown in the table.

From the information above and in the table, answer the questions below.

Participant	Height (cm)	Ear lobes
1	160	free
2	154	attached
3	174	free
4	163	free
5	152	attached
6	170	free

↑ Free ear lobe

↑ Attached ear lobe

a) What is the difference in height between the tallest and shortest person? Show your working. *(1 mark)*

b) The students wanted their investigation to be scientific.

   i) State **one** way in which their investigation was a fair test. *(1 mark)*

   ii) How could they make their results more reproducible? *(1 mark)*

c) Which of these variations (ear lobes and height) is an example of continuous variation? *(1 mark)*

d) Complete the sentences using some of the words below:

   sexual   asexual   identical   different   environment

   Variation results from _____ reproduction when two parents produce offspring which have _____ genes. The _____ can also cause variation. *(3 marks)*

Go online for answers
Online

Genetic disorders and gene therapy

Sometimes a mutation can result in a 'faulty' gene, as a result of which the body does not function properly. The person has a **genetic disorder**, which can also be inherited by descendants.

Genetic disorders

Revised

An example of a genetic disorder is the disease cystic fibrosis, where the lungs and digestive system are clogged with thick mucus.

- Cystic fibrosis is caused by a recessive allele. (In this example we will call the normal allele N and the cystic fibrosis allele n.)
- People who are heterozygous (Nn) show no symptoms of cystic fibrosis.
- People who are homozygous recessive (nn) have cystic fibrosis. They will have received a cystic fibrosis allele from both of their parents.
- The heterozygotes can pass on the cystic fibrosis allele to their children, and are called **carriers**.

The Punnett square below shows how two normal parents can have a child with cystic fibrosis.

Parental phenotype	Normal	x	Normal
Parental genotype	Nn		Nm
Gametes	N or n		N or n

		Male	
Gametes		**N**	**n**
Female	**N**	NN	Nn
	n	Nn	(nn)——cystic fibrosis sufferer

In principle, one in four of the children will suffer from cystic fibrosis (see also page 29). It is likely that half of the couple's children will carry the disease but not suffer from it.

Other examples of genetic disorders include haemophilia, Huntington's chorea, and red-green colour blindness.

Gene therapy

Revised

Scientists are learning how to transfer genes from one individual to another. It may be possible in the future to delete a faulty gene and replace it with a normal one, and so cure genetic disorders such as cystic fibrosis. Treatments are being researched but none are available yet. Some of the issues surrounding gene therapy are:

- Most of the treatments being trialled involve altering the genes of specific cells, but this will only provide a temporary cure because the modified cells will die and be replaced with faulty ones again. The patient will need regular treatment.

- The clinical trials have not so far been very successful (though the research is still at an early stage).

- The treatment is likely to be very expensive, and may initially be available only in developed countries and to rich individuals.

- If genes can be replaced in embryos, the change would be permanent. This could allow unscrupulous people to swap genes that are nothing to do with disease (e.g. controlling what eye colour their child has) and create 'designer babies'.

- Some people with certain genetic disorders do not like their condition to be treated as a 'disease' because they think it devalues them.

- If successful, gene therapy has the potential to save many lives and improve the quality of people's lives.

Examiner tip

Some religious groups believe that science should never 'play God' and experiment with or alter the human body. There are a number of issues in the GCSE Science specification which fall into this category. In general, if asked for objections to a development, you will not get marks for objections that are purely religious and are not specific to the topic.

Check your understanding   Tested

31 The diagram below shows the inheritance of cystic fibrosis in a family.

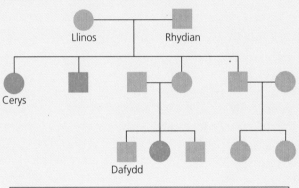

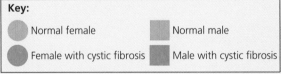

Key:

⬤ Normal female   ⬛ Normal male

⬤ Female with cystic fibrosis   ⬛ Male with cystic fibrosis

a) Using **N** to represent the normal allele and **n** to represent the allele for cystic fibrosis, state the genotypes of the grandparents, Llinos and Rhydian. *(2 marks)*

b) State the genotype of Cerys. *(1 mark)*

c) State the **two** possible genotypes that could occur in Dafydd. *(2 marks)*

32 Gene therapy involves replacing faulty genes with healthy ones. It has great potential in treating genetic disorders, but the research is very expensive. State **two** reasons why some people object to this research. *(2 marks)*

Go online for answers   Online

Evolution and natural selection

Evolution is the gradual change of species over time, resulting in the formation of new species and the extinction of some others. **Natural selection** is the generally accepted mechanism for the evolution of new species. As a result of natural selection, animals and plants become better adapted to their environment.

The theory of natural selection

Revised

This theory was proposed by Charles Darwin. It is generally accepted by scientists, although some modifications and developments have occurred as a result of later discoveries in genetics and molecular biology.

The theory can be summarised as follows:

- Populations of all living organisms show **variation**. Heritable variation is the basis of evolution.

- Not all individuals in a population can survive, so there is **competition** for survival.

- Some variants within a population will be **better adapted** to the environment, and will be better equipped to survive. This is sometimes called **survival of the fittest**.

- Those that survive long enough to breed will pass on their genes to the next generation.

- As the individuals who are better adapted have a better chance of survival, their genes are more likely to be passed on.

- The next generation will have more individuals with the better adapted genes.

- Over a long period of time, the population becomes better and better adapted to their environment, provided the environment does not change.

- Organisms that are less well suited to their environment, or that cannot adapt quickly enough when the environment changes, will become **extinct**.

> **Examiner tip**
>
> In questions about natural selection, don't forget about the competition for survival within a population. This stage is often missed out by students in their answers.

Examples of evolution

Revised

Evolution is happening all the time. About 50 years ago, warfarin was a very successful rat poison. It was so successful that almost everyone trying to get rid of rats used it. Modern rats are mostly resistant to warfarin, due to the process below:

- Some rats were naturally resistant to warfarin.

- When warfarin was used, only the resistant rats survived.

- Warfarin was used so much that nearly all the non-resistant rats were killed, leaving only the resistant ones.

- Warfarin resistance is genetic, so the offspring of resistant rats were mostly resistant.

- The same process occurred over several generations, until nearly all rats in the UK population were warfarin-resistant.

Scientists are worried that a similar thing may happen if we keep using the same antibiotics to treat disease. The bacteria may become resistant, and the antibiotics will be useless. To try to prevent this, doctors avoid prescribing antibiotics unless they are essential, and use a wide range of different antibiotics.

Examiner tip

One possible answer to Question **33** part **b) i)** might be 'natural selection', but as that is used in the question it cannot be the answer required (that would be too easy!). You need to think of an alternative answer.

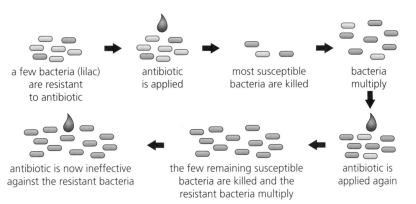

a few bacteria (lilac) are resistant to antibiotic → antibiotic is applied → most susceptible bacteria are killed → bacteria multiply

antibiotic is now ineffective against the resistant bacteria ← the few remaining susceptible bacteria are killed and the resistant bacteria multiply ← antibiotic is applied again

↑ The evolution of resistance to antibiotics in bacteria. Note that in reality many more generations would be required before full resistance evolved

Check your understanding

Tested

33 Male guppies are colourful tropical fish.

- Their colours occur in various patterns.
- The patterns are controlled by genes.
- Some patterns are more commonly seen than others.
- Predators find it more difficult to target the rarer, most colourful patterns but easily find the less colourful patterns.
- Female guppies select the most colourful males to breed.

a) Use this information to explain how natural selection results in male guppies existing in such a rich variety of colours. *(5 marks)*

b) This example of natural selection could be used to explain a theory put forward by a famous scientist in 1859 in his book *The Origin of Species*.

i) Name the theory. *(1 mark)*

ii) Name the famous scientist who developed the theory. *(1 mark)*

34 Giraffes feed on the leaves of tall trees. They have adapted to their habitat by evolving long necks and long legs. This has happened by the process of **natural selection**. Explain how natural selection could have resulted in an increase in the length of the giraffes' necks. *(6 marks QWC)*

Go online for answers

Online

Sensitivity in plants and animals

Sensitivity

Revised

All animals and plants are **sensitive** – they can detect changes in their environment. Any change that is detected is called a **stimulus**. If necessary, they then **respond** to stimuli in various ways.

Sense organs in animals

Revised

Sense organs in animals are groups of receptor cells, which respond to specific stimuli. Some examples of sense organs are shown in the diagram.

When the cells of a sense organ are stimulated, they relay this information along nerve cells (**neurons**) to the **central nervous system** (the brain and spinal cord). Nerves contain large numbers of neurons, bundled together. The message travels in the form of an **electrical impulse**. The central nervous system can coordinate the information and send outgoing impulses to an effector, which can cause a response.

stimulus $\longrightarrow$ sense organ $\longrightarrow$ coordinator $\longrightarrow$ effector $\longrightarrow$ response

The whole process of responding to a stimulus can be very quick. The time between the stimulus and the response is called the **reaction time**.

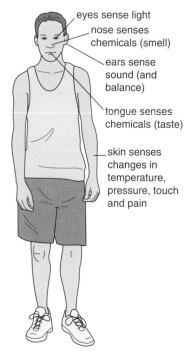

eyes sense light

nose senses chemicals (smell)

ears sense sound (and balance)

tongue senses chemicals (taste)

skin senses changes in temperature, pressure, touch and pain

↑ Sense organs in humans

Sensitivity in plants

Revised

Plants are also sensitive to changes in their environment, mostly relating to light and gravity. Plants cannot move around, but they respond by the way they grow. It is important that when seeds germinate, they grow the right way up. To ensure this, roots always grow towards the pull of gravity (downwards). The stem will grow away from gravity. The response to gravity is called **gravitropism**. Roots are **positively gravitropic**, and stems are **negatively gravitropic**.

The response to light is called phototropism. Plants need light to carry out photosynthesis, and cannot survive without it. The stems of plants are **positively phototropic**, so that they always grow towards the light. This ensures that they get the maximum amount of light from their environment.

Plants have no nerves and the tropisms are controlled by plant **hormones** (chemicals which can move around the plant and cause a response).

Examiner tip

You will not have done the experiment in Question **36**, but that does not matter. Apart from part **c)**, this question is testing data handling skills (*How Science Works*) and not factual knowledge. There are always a number of questions like this in every paper and it is important that you develop these skills if you are going to get the best grades.

35 a) Complete the table of human senses using some of
the words below: *(3 marks)*

eye   tongue   hearing   taste   sound   light

Body organ	Stimulus	Sense
eye	light	sight
tongue	chemical	taste
ear	sound	hearing

b) Complete the passage below using words from the list to
complete the sentences. *(5 marks)*

brain   receptor   impulses   electrical   hormone   respond

Sense organs are groups of _____ cells. They _____ to stimuli
and relay information as _____ signals called nerve _____ to the
_____.

36 Scientists did an experiment to gain information about phototropism in plants.
The experiment is shown in the diagram below. After two days, the scientists
recorded if the stems had bent towards the light.

light

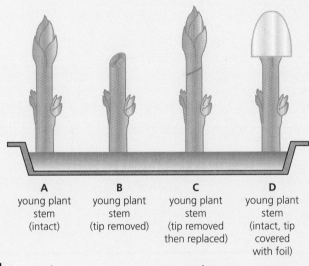

	A	B	C	D
	young plant stem (intact)	young plant stem (tip removed)	young plant stem (tip removed then replaced)	young plant stem (intact, tip covered with foil)
Did stem bend towards the light?	✓	✗	✓	✗

a) State which of the conclusions listed below is justified from the results of
this experiment: *(1 mark)*

A The light is detected by the tip of the stem.

B The bending is caused by a hormone.

C Damaging the plant stops the response.

D Bending occurs when the tip of the stem is present.

b) The scientists concluded that the message cannot be relayed by
structures like nerves. Explain how the evidence from this
experiment supports this conclusion. *(2 marks)*

c) Plant stems grow towards light but away from gravity. State the name
given to a response to gravity. *(1 mark)*

Homeostasis and hormones

The body needs to keep certain conditions inside it constant. This is done by special chemicals called **hormones**.

Keeping control
Revised

The body works by means of chemical reactions. Chemical reactions are affected by a number of factors, such as **temperature**, **pH** and the **concentration** of the reagents. For the body to work properly, these factors have to be kept relatively constant. The main things that the body regulates are:

- **Temperature**, so that the reactions do not go too fast or too slow. The enzymes which control all the reactions in the body are affected by temperature.

- **Water content**, so that reagents don't get too dilute or too concentrated.

- **Blood sugar levels**. Glucose is necessary for energy, but damages cells if it becomes too concentrated, so keeping the level steady is important. Glucose levels will also affect the concentrations of body fluids, and if these become too concentrated, harm can result. Failure of the body to control sugar levels results in a disease, called diabetes, which can be fatal if not treated.

> **Examiner tip**
>
> For GCSE Science, you have to know how the body controls temperature and sugar levels. The name given to keeping body conditions constant is 'homeostasis'. You do not need to know the name, but you do need to understand the concept.

Hormones
Revised

Hormones are chemical messengers, which are produced in certain places in the body but have their effects in other places. Hormones are proteins, and they are carried around the body in the blood.

Negative feedback
Revised

The way in which hormones control the level of factors in the body is by a process known as negative feedback. Negative feedback works like this:

- If a factor increases, a chain of events is set in motion which causes the factor to be lowered again.

- If the factor gets too low, another chain of events is set in motion which causes the factor to be raised.

An example of negative feedback is shown below. It shows how blood sugar levels are controlled by two hormones, insulin and glucagon.

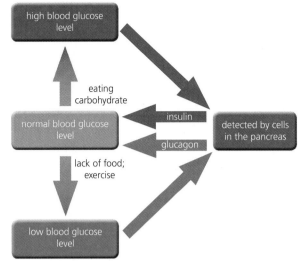

↑ **Negative feedback control of blood glucose levels**

Examiner tip

The two questions below are very different in their demand. Question **37** is much easier than Question **38**. The questions get more difficult as you progress through the paper. The first questions on a foundation paper will be quite easy, but the later questions in the higher-tier paper will be very demanding. It is very important you don't make careless mistakes in the early questions, because you are then giving easy marks away.

Check your understanding

Tested

37 Complete the passage below, using some of the words supplied. *(5 marks)*

single   nervous system   many   electrical   temperature   blood

chemical   blood sugar level   nerves   hormones

The human body has processes which keep key factors inside it relatively constant. One of these factors is _____. Control is carried out by _____. These are _____ messengers which are carried in the _____ to _____ organs.

38 The graph below shows fluctuations in a person's blood sugar (glucose) and insulin levels over a period of time. Insulin is a hormone which reduces blood sugar.

glucose level

insulin level

level in blood

time

a) Describe the relationship between the glucose level and the insulin level in the blood. *(2 marks)*

b) This is an example of negative feedback. State the meaning of the term 'negative feedback'. *(1 mark)*

c) Explain how the data indicates that negative feedback is occurring. *(2 marks)*

Go online for answers

Online

Glucose control and diabetes

What is diabetes?

Normally, the human body keeps the levels of glucose in the blood within a restricted range. In certain people, the control mechanism fails and as a result they get diabetes. The control can be artificially restored by regular injections of the hormone insulin.

Control of blood glucose levels

When we eat food containing carbohydrates, the level of sugar (glucose) in the blood will rise. To stop it rising beyond a certain limit, the **pancreas** produces a hormone, **insulin**, which allows the glucose to be used by the cells. It also causes any excess to be converted into insoluble **glycogen** in the **liver**, which then stores it for future use.

> **Examiner tip**
>
> If you are sitting the higher-tier paper, you need to know a little more about the mechanism involved in the control of blood glucose levels. This is covered in the previous section on 'Negative feedback' (pages 40–41).

Diabetes

Certain people do not produce enough insulin. As a result, blood glucose could rise to fatal levels. The essential facts about diabetes that you need to know are:

● If it is suspected that a patient has diabetes, the doctor will ask for a urine sample and test it for sugar. The presence of sugar in the urine means that the patient has diabetes.

● Testing urine for sugar is normally done using testing sticks with a chemical on them which changes colour in the presence of glucose.

● An earlier test was to do a Benedict's test for sugar. This involves boiling the urine with Benedict's solution, which is a dilute solution of copper sulfate. When boiled, the colour changes from clear blue to a cloudy orange or brick red indicating the presence of glucose.

● In healthy people, glucose is re-absorbed from the urine in the kidneys. Untreated diabetics have such high levels of glucose, the mechanism cannot cope.

● Diabetics have to inject insulin before meals. They then have to eat just enough carbohydrate in that meal to balance the insulin injected.

● In order to know how much insulin they need to inject, diabetic patients will often test their blood glucose level before a meal, using a blood testing meter.

● Eating carbohydrates raises the level of sugar in the blood; exercise or lack of food reduces the level of glucose. Diabetics have to take account of such factors when deciding how much insulin to inject.

● Some diabetics are now treated by having a transplant of pancreatic tissue to replace their damaged pancreatic cells.

The facts listed on the previous page apply to the type of diabetes known as 'type 1'. There is also a 'type 2' diabetes, which is treated by diet or tablets rather than by injecting insulin (see page 49).

↑ People with type 1 diabetes have to inject themselves with insulin, sometimes several times a day

> **Examiner tip**
>
> Questions on diabetes very often ask you to interpret blood sugar data (either from a table or from a graph). You will be expected to know the factors which increase and decrease blood glucose levels, so make sure you are confident in handling such data.

Check your understanding   Tested

39 a) Name the organ in the body which produces insulin. *(1 mark)*

b) How does insulin reduce the concentration of glucose in the blood? *(1 mark)*

c) In which organ in the body does this take place? *(1 mark)*

40 Owen has diabetes. He measures his blood glucose level using a monitor.

Owen injects himself with a measured dose of insulin before each meal. The dose depends on his blood glucose reading. If the glucose reading is high, Owen injects a higher dose of insulin.

Owen monitors his blood glucose regularly throughout each day. He records his readings in a diary. He tries to keep his blood glucose reading within the normal range of 4.0–7.0 (mmol/l).

The table below shows a section from Owen's diary over a 3 day period.

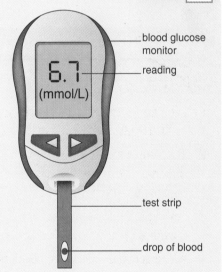

	Owen's blood glucose level (mmol/l)						
Date	Before breakfast	2 hours after breakfast	Before midday meal	2 hours after midday meal	Before evening meal	2 hours after evening meal	Before bed
29 Jan	7.0		9.1	6.8	4.3	(14.2)	12.9
30 Jan	9.0	7.5	7.1		6.2		7.9
31 Jan	5.3		7.4		(2.9)		8.2

a) Suggest a reason for:

   i) the high reading 2 hours after the evening meal on 29 Jan (circled). *(1 mark)*

   ii) the low reading before the evening meal on 31 Jan (circled). *(1 mark)*

b) Suggest why Owen always measures his blood glucose before bedtime. *(1 mark)*

Go online for answers   Online

The skin and temperature control

The structure of the skin

The diagram shows the structure of the skin. The labels that could be tested in the exam are:

● hair
● erector muscle
● sweat gland
● sweat pore
● sweat duct
● blood vessels.

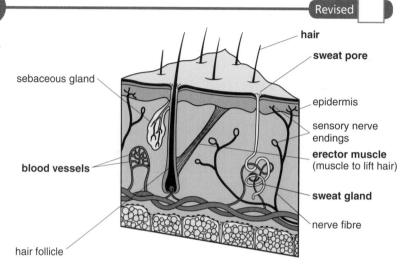

sebaceous gland

blood vessels

hair follicle

hair

sweat pore

epidermis

sensory nerve endings

erector muscle (muscle to lift hair)

sweat gland

nerve fibre

⬆ **A section through human skin**

Controlling temperature

The skin is an important organ in controlling temperature. It does this in various ways.

The blood vessels can change their diameter

When blood flows near the surface, heat is lost to the air. The blood vessels in the skin can widen to allow more blood to flow to the surface, or narrow to restrict surface blood flow. In warm conditions, the blood vessels open; more blood flows to the surface and more heat is lost, so that the animal cools down. In cold conditions, the vessels constrict to cut the blood flow, so less heat is lost. This does not warm the animal, but it does stop it losing more heat. This change in the flow of blood in the skin explains why we get red in the heat, but pale in cold weather.

The hairs can stand up or lie flat

The erector muscles in the skin can contract to raise the hairs. The air trapped between the erect hairs acts as an insulating layer, and stops the skin losing heat. This happens in cold conditions, and the insulation the raised hair/fur provides limits the heat that is lost from the skin. When it is warm, the skin needs to lose heat. The erector muscles relax, the hairs are lowered, and there is no longer an insulating layer of air. As a result, the skin will lose more heat.

The skin produces sweat

In hot conditions, the skin produces sweat. When the sweat evaporates from the skin, it requires heat in order to change the liquid sweat into a vapour. This heat is drawn from the skin, and so cools it down.

Shivering

There is another mechanism, not involving the skin, which warms us up in cold weather. We shiver, and the heat generated by the contracting muscles warms the blood.

The table below summarises the mechanisms used to control body temperature.

Hot conditions	Cold conditions
Blood flows to the skin surface	Blood is kept deep in the skin
Hairs lie flat	Hairs stand erect and create an insulating layer
Sweat is produced	Little or no sweat is produced
No shivering occurs	Shivering occurs

Examiner tip

Remember that with Quality of Written Communication questions like Question **42** the examiners will be looking for clear explanations. If you get the basic facts right but your explanation is not clear or lacks detail, you may lose marks. See pages 110–111 for more help answering QWC questions.

Check your understanding

Tested ☐

41 The diagram shows the structure of the human skin.

a) Using the terms below identify labels A, B, C and D on the diagram. *(4 marks)*

sweat duct   muscle   blood capillary   sweat pore   hair

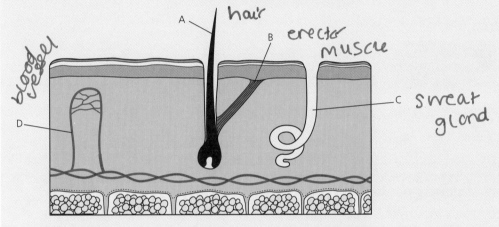

b) Complete the table below to show how the skin helps to reduce heat loss in a **cold** environment. *(3 marks)*

Structure	How heat loss is reduced
Hair	
	Becomes narrower (constricts)
Sweat gland	

c) In cold weather shivering occurs. How is this helpful? *(1 mark)*

42 Birds, like mammals, can control their body temperature. Birds have feathers in their skin, whereas mammals have hair. In the winter, but not in summer, birds are seen to 'fluff out' their feathers. Suggest how fluffing out their feathers may help birds to control their body temperature. *(6 marks QWC)*

Go online for answers

Online

Food, energy and health

Energy content of foods Revised

We eat food to provide us with energy and the raw materials for growth. Different foods provide differing amounts of energy.

● **Carbohydrates** provide energy that can be accessed quickly.

● **Fats** provide more energy per gram than carbohydrates, but more slowly.

● **Proteins** are not normally used for energy – they provide materials for growth and repair.

If there is more energy in the food we eat than we need, our bodies store the excess.

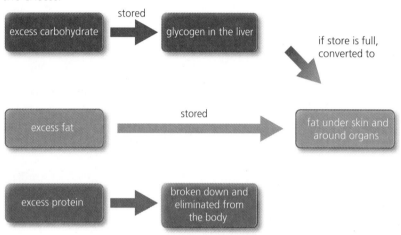

Continually eating too much carbohydrate or fat results in a lot of fat being stored, and the person becomes overweight.

Measuring the energy in food Revised

When food is burnt, the energy in it is released. This energy can be measured by burning the food to heat water, and measuring the temperature rise. The energy of the food in joules can be calculated.

1 calorie = amount of energy needed to raise the temperature of 1 cm³ of water by 1 °C.

1 calorie = 4.2 joules

The energy in 1 g of food can be calculated using this formula:

> **Examiner tip**
> You may be asked to use this formula in an exam question, but it will always be given – you will not be expected to remember it.

$$\text{energy in 1 g food} = \frac{\text{volume of water heated (cm}^3\text{)} \times \text{rise in temperature (°C)} \times 4.2}{\text{mass of food (g)}}$$

Food and health Revised

All foods can be safely eaten, but an excess of certain components in food can damage health. The table on the next page shows three food components that are a cause for concern.

Information about the components of packaged food can be found on food labels. The ingredients are listed (in order of quantity) and there is often a nutrition table showing the amount of different food types in 100 g of the product.

Component	Concern	Associated health problems
Sugar	High energy food which many people over-eat	Obesity, which can lead to heart disease and other conditions
	Remains on teeth and provides food for bacteria	Tooth decay
Fat	High energy food which many people over-eat	Obesity, which can lead to heart disease and other conditions
	Animal fats form cholesterol in the body, which is deposited on the inside of blood vessels	Heart disease
Additives	Additives in food have all been tested and are generally safe, but some people react badly to certain additives. Salt is a common additive in many foods	Hyperactivity in children Asthma Allergies Headaches High blood pressure (salt)

Check your understanding
Tested

43 The apparatus on the right was set up to measure the energy content of a piece of food.

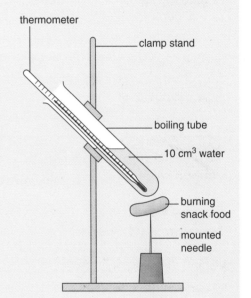

a) State **two** measurements that you must take in order to find the energy content of the food. *(2 marks)*

b) If you were comparing the energy content of two different foods state **one** other measurement that must be taken. *(1 mark)*

44 The table below shows the contents of three drinks and their use in the body. Use the information **in the table** to answer the questions that follow.

	Use in the body	Whole milk (500 cm³)	Skimmed milk (500 cm³)	Fruit juice (500 cm³)
Energy value (kJ)	–	1315	1045	513
Protein (g)	Builds and repairs organs	16	18	3.0
Carbohydrate (mainly sugars) (g)	Provides energy	23.5	24	40.0
Fat (g)	Energy store	18	5.5	0
Calcium (mg)	Healthy bones and teeth	335	350	0

a) i) How much more energy (in kJ) is there in 500 cm³ of whole milk than in 500 cm³ of skimmed milk? *(1 mark)*

ii) A carton of whole milk contains 1000 cm³. How much energy (in kJ) is contained in the carton? *(1 mark)*

b) Whole milk is changed into skimmed milk by a process called skimming.
  i) What is removed when the milk is skimmed? *(1 mark)*
  ii) What type of milk should a person choose in order to lose weight? *(1 mark)*

c) Give **two** reasons why a dentist suggests you should drink milk instead of fruit juice. *(2 marks)*

Go online for answers
Online

Lifestyle and health

A person's health is affected in various ways by their lifestyle. Some choices (for example regular exercise and eating a healthy diet) can benefit health, but others (poor eating choices, lack of exercise, and alcohol and drug abuse) can lead to serious health problems.

Drug abuse   Revised

A drug is a substance which alters the way the body works. Nearly all drugs do this in many different ways, only some of which were intended by the user. The other effects are called **side-effects**. Human beings take a wide variety of drugs, and they can be of great benefit in treating disease. However, when drugs are taken in excess the side-effects can be serious and this is referred to as **drug abuse**.

Drugs affect the chemical processes in the body. This can have physical effects and, if the processes in the brain are affected, mental effects too. Some drugs cause physical addiction – if you stop taking the drug, unpleasant **withdrawal effects** appear until you take another dose.

Some examples of the effects of drug abuse are listed below.

Drug	Effects
Cannabis	Dizziness and sickness, panic, hunger, high blood pressure, psychological problems
Amphetamines	Addiction, increased heart rate, nausea, low blood pressure, psychological problems
Cocaine	Similar to amphetamines but much more addictive and more likely to lead to psychological problems including depression and anxiety, risk of heart attack
Heroin	Slows the body down, effective painkiller, highly addictive, psychological problems
Anabolic steroids	Build muscle, increased risk of liver failure, heart disease and stroke; can cause trans-gender effects (e.g. breast development in males, facial hair in females)

Examiner tip

The drugs and effects given in the table are examples only – you will not be asked about any **specific** drug (apart from alcohol) in the exam. You might be asked to give an example of the effects of a drug on the body, in which case you could use any of those above.

Alcohol abuse   Revised

Alcohol is a drug, and like other drugs it can have harmful effects if it is taken in large quantities or very frequently.

Alcohol **slows body processes down**, and so having an alcoholic drink will make people react more slowly. This can be dangerous when driving, operating machinery, or doing anything which requires concentration in order to avoid danger. Alcohol is processed in the liver, but it is a poison, so prolonged or excessive use can cause serious **liver damage**.

Excessive alcohol consumption can also lead to diseases of the **kidney** and the **stomach**.

Obesity results from a combination of an unhealthy diet and lack of exercise. It has wide-ranging effects on health and will increase the risk of the following:

● heart disease

● some cancers

● high blood pressure

● type 2 diabetes.

In the section on 'Glucose control and diabetes' (pages 42–43), we looked at **type 1 diabetes**, which is not linked with being overweight. Type 2 diabetes tends to develop in middle age, and is usually controlled with tablets rather than by insulin injections.

45 The table shows how some lifestyle choices can affect health. Use the information to answer the questions.

a) Which food substance can increase the risk of heart disease? *(1 mark)*

b) How can a person reduce the risk of obesity and stroke? *(2 marks)*

c) Name **two** organs of the body in which disease can develop because of drinking too much alcohol. *(1 mark)*

Lifestyle choice	Increased health risk
Eating too much high energy food	Obesity
High fat diet	Heart disease
Too much salt in diet	Stroke
Drinking too much alcohol	Kidney disease Gastritis in stomach Cirrhosis of the liver

46 Blood samples were taken from a person before drinking alcohol and every hour for 5 hours afterwards. The results for the concentration of alcohol in the blood are shown in the graph on the right.

Use the graph to answer the following questions.

a) What was the concentration of alcohol in the blood after 1½ hours? *(1 mark)*

It is illegal to drive if the concentration of alcohol is above 80 mg/100 cm³.

b) Use the graph to find out for how long this person would be over the limit of 80 mg/100 cm³. *(1 mark)*

c) Why does drinking alcohol increase the chance of having an accident? Select the correct answer. *(1 mark)*

A It is a stimulant.

B It causes slurred speech.

C It slows down reactions.

D It cools the body.

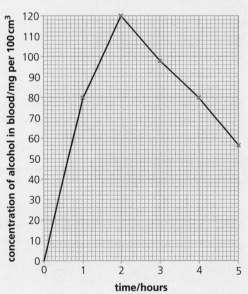

Treatment of disease

Science plays a major role in keeping people healthy. It does this in the following ways:

- Finding ways of curing or treating diseases and conditions.
- Discovering the causes of disease and advising people on how to prevent them.
- Preventing disease by developing and administering vaccines.

Drugs to treat disease   Revised

Diseases can be treated by developing medicinal drugs or by other therapies. There are various issues surrounding drug treatments.

- Drug treatments usually have **side-effects** which can be serious.
- Drugs require **large scale**, **rigorous testing**. This is expensive and takes a long time. The testing involves risk management, weighing the benefits against any drawbacks.
- Many drugs are **very expensive**. Health service administrators have limited budgets and have to make decisions about whether drug treatments are affordable and cost-effective.

Ethical issues   Revised

Examples of some of the issues involved in treating patients with drugs are outlined below.

- Some expensive drugs do not cure, but prolong life. Buying this drug to treat patients may cause other treatment programmes or facilities to be cut back.
- Some drugs are only effective in a small number of people. Treating people who turn out to be unaffected by the drug would waste a lot of money.
- Sometimes a new drug is only slightly more effective than an old one, but is far more expensive.

Animal testing   Revised

New drugs are first tested on laboratory animals to look for side-effects, before being tested on humans. The experiments may be painful in some cases or reduce the animal's quality of life. Many people object to animal testing, but medical researchers insist that it is sometimes necessary. People who are against animal testing argue:

- It causes suffering in the animals.
- The benefits to humans are not proven. The animals are not human and so their reactions to drugs may be different.
- There are alternative methods that could be used.

The arguments put forward by some scientists for animal testing are:

- Licensed scientists always try to minimise any suffering to the animals, which are generally well looked after.
- The research brings benefits to humans which cannot be obtained by other methods.

Alternatives to animal testing are:

- Using computer models.
- Testing on tissue cultures of animal cells rather than whole animals.
- Theoretical and statistical studies of diseases in humans could avoid some of the animal tests.

Examiner tip

This section of the specification does not have many facts to learn. Exam questions usually involve using information from text, handling data or giving an opinion.

Check your understanding   Tested

47 Read the following information.

A monkey is shown above. Monkeys are closely related to humans. Scientists discussed the use of monkeys in laboratory work.

Scientists in group 1 said:	Scientists in group 2 said:
It is essential to use monkeys in testing new drugs.	Tests cause monkeys distress and should be avoided.
New drugs for strokes, AIDS, kidney failure and other human diseases have been developed.	The number of tests on monkeys should be reduced as soon as possible.
In future, there should be far fewer tests on monkeys.	The tests could be done using tissue cultures or computers.

a) Answer the following questions **using the information given above only**.

   i) For what purpose do group 1 scientists say they need to use monkeys? *(1 mark)*

   ii) Give **two** human diseases which can now be treated. *(1 mark)*

   iii) State **one** reason given by the group 2 scientists for not using monkeys. *(1 mark)*

   iv) State **two** alternative methods for doing tests. *(1 mark)*

b) Suggest **one** reason why people may worry more about using monkeys in experiments rather than other animals. *(1 mark)*

c) Give **one** way in which both groups of scientists were in agreement. *(1 mark)*

Go online for answers   Online

Atoms, elements and the Periodic Table

- **Elements** are the basic building blocks of matter.
- Elements cannot be broken into anything simpler by chemical means.
- Each element has its own symbol.
- Elements are made up of **atoms**, and all the atoms of an element are of the same type.
- The atomic structure of an element determines its position in the Periodic Table of the elements.

Atomic structure

- Each atom contains a small, positively charged central region called the **nucleus**.
- The nucleus is made up of two types of particle – **protons** (which have a positive charge) and **neutrons** (which have no charge).
- Light, negatively charged **electrons** orbit around the nucleus.

cloud of negative electrons

positive nucleus

↑ **Model of the structure of an atom**

- Every atom of a particular element has the same number of protons. The number of protons is known as the **atomic number**, and every element has a different atomic number.
- The mass of an atom of an element is called its **relative atomic mass**.
- The nucleus contains nearly all the mass of the atom.

The Periodic Table

The Periodic Table is a table showing all the known elements, arranged in a logical way that allows chemists to predict the properties of individual elements.

The rows of the Periodic Table are called **periods**, and the columns are called **groups**. Note that some of the elements in the middle, **the transition elements**, have no group number. Sometimes, you may see numbers on all the columns (1–18), but that is not the system used in the GCSE exam.

> **Examiner tip**
>
> Do not attempt to memorise the Periodic Table! It is always given on the exam paper. For each element, it will give you the element name, symbol, mass number and atomic number. Remember that this may be useful even in questions that are not actually about the Periodic Table.

Mendeléev

The first useful 'periodic table' was developed by **Dmitri Mendeléev** in 1869. He noticed that when the elements were arranged in order of relative atomic mass, their properties showed recurring patterns. However, there appeared to be gaps in the sequence in some places. He concluded that these gaps represented elements that had yet to be discovered. Using his periodic table, Mendeléev successfully predicted the properties of some of these undiscovered elements. The elements are now arranged in order of **atomic number**, not atomic mass.

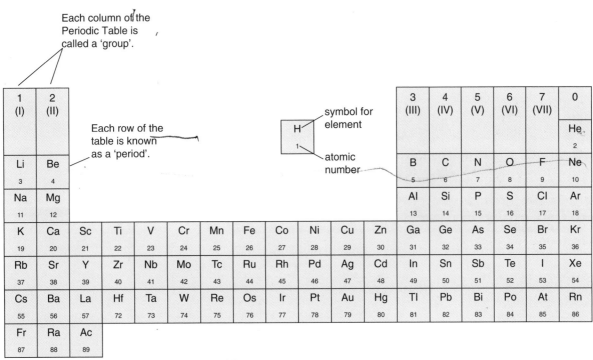

Each column of the Periodic Table is called a 'group'.

Each row of the table is known as a 'period'.

symbol for element

atomic number

1 (I)	2 (II)											3 (III)	4 (IV)	5 (V)	6 (VI)	7 (VII)	0
					H 1												He 2
Li 3	Be 4											B 5	C 6	N 7	O 8	F 9	Ne 10
Na 11	Mg 12											Al 13	Si 14	P 15	S 16	Cl 17	Ar 18
K 19	Ca 20	Sc 21	Ti 22	V 23	Cr 24	Mn 25	Fe 26	Co 27	Ni 28	Cu 29	Zn 30	Ga 31	Ge 32	As 33	Se 34	Br 35	Kr 36
Rb 37	Sr 38	Y 39	Zr 40	Nb 41	Mo 42	Tc 43	Ru 44	Rh 45	Pd 46	Ag 47	Cd 48	In 49	Sn 50	Sb 51	Te 52	I 53	Xe 54
Cs 55	Ba 56	La 57	Hf 72	Ta 73	W 74	Re 75	Os 76	Ir 77	Pt 78	Au 79	Hg 80	Tl 81	Pb 82	Bi 83	Po 84	At 85	Rn 86
Fr 87	Ra 88	Ac 89															

⬆ The Periodic Table of the elements

Tested

Use the Periodic Table of the elements shown above to help you when answering these questions.

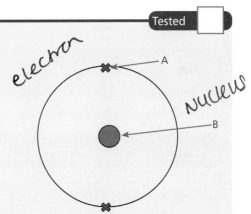

electron

nucleus

A

B

1 The diagram shows the structure of an atom of helium (He).

   a) Name the parts of the atom labelled A and B. (2 marks)

   b) Give the symbol of the element that is in the same group as helium in the Periodic Table but in Period 2. (1 mark)

2 The following table shows the 'periodic table' that was published by Mendeléev in 1869.

Period	Group							
	1	2	3	4	5	6	7	0
1	H							
2	Li	Be	B	C	N	O	F	
3	Na	Mg	Al	Si	P	S	Cl	
4	K	Ca	•	Ti	V	Cr	Mn	Fe Co Ni
	Cu	Zn	•	•	As	Se	Br	
5	Rb	Sr	Y	Zr	Nb	Mo	•	Ru Rh Pd
	Ag	Cd	In	Sn	Sb	Te	I	

   a) Give a reason why Mendeléev used • in some of the boxes. (1 mark)

   b) Name **two** elements present in Group 1 of Mendeléev's table that are not in Group 1 of the present day Periodic Table. (1 mark)

   c) Mendeléev arranged the elements in order of increasing atomic mass. State how the elements are arranged in the present day Periodic Table. (1 mark)

Go online for answers

Online

Distinguishing metals and non-metals

The position of an element in the Periodic Table gives us information about its properties. There are distinct trends in properties as you go either across, or up and down the table. **Metals** have similar properties which distinguish them from **non-metals**, and so metals and non-metals are found in different parts of the Periodic Table.

The properties of metals and non-metals

Revised

The table below shows the different properties of metals and non-metals.

Metals	Non-metals
Good conductors of heat and electricity	Poor conductors of heat and electricity
Malleable (bendable)	Non-malleable
Ductile (can be stretched into wires)	Non-ductile
Hard, dense and shiny	Soft/brittle solids, low density, not shiny, many are gases at room temperature
High melting and boiling points	Low melting and boiling points

These properties are generalisations, so there are occasional exceptions (for example, lead is not ductile, and carbon (in the form of graphite) is a good conductor of electricity).

Metals and non-metals in the Periodic Table

Revised

The Periodic Table below is coloured to indicate where metals and non-metals are found.

1 (I)	2 (II)											3 (III)	4 (IV)	5 (V)	6 (VI)	7 (VII)	0
							H 1										He 2
Li 3	Be 4											B 5	C 6	N 7	O 8	F 9	Ne 10
Na 11	Mg 12											Al 13	Si 14	P 15	S 16	Cl 17	Ar 18
K 19	Ca 20	Sc 21	Ti 22	V 23	Cr 24	Mn 25	Fe 26	Co 27	Ni 28	Cu 29	Zn 30	Ga 31	Ge 32	As 33	Se 34	Br 35	Kr 36
Rb 37	Sr 38	Y 39	Zr 40	Nb 41	Mo 42	Tc 43	Ru 44	Rh 45	Pd 46	Ag 47	Cd 48	In 49	Sn 50	Sb 51	Te 52	I 53	Xe 54
Cs 55	Ba 56	La 57	Hf 72	Ta 73	W 74	Re 75	Os 76	Ir 77	Pt 78	Au 79	Hg 80	Tl 81	Pb 82	Bi 83	Po 84	At 85	Rn 86
Fr 87	Ra 88	Ac 89															

⬆ The modern Periodic Table; metals are shaded green and non-metals purple

On the border between metals and non-metals lie some elements with intermediate properties, for example silicon, which is a **semi-conductor** and is sometimes referred to as a 'metalloid'.

Predictions using the Periodic Table

There are distinct trends in properties within each group of the Periodic Table, and these trends can be used to predict the properties of elements. For example, caesium is a very highly reactive metal in Group 1 and its melting point cannot be measured by conventional means. However, it can be predicted by looking at the melting points of other metals in the group.

Examiner tip

Caesium is used as an example here. You do not have to learn about caesium, but you may be asked to make predictions about the properties of an element by using data from the other elements in the group.

Element	Melting point (°C)
Lithium (Li)	180
Sodium (Na)	98
Potassium (K)	64
Rubidium (Rb)	39
Caesium (Cs)	28*

* predicted from the m.p. of other elements in the group

Check your understanding

3 Rubidium is a metallic element, with the properties shown in the table:

   a) State **one** property of rubidium which identifies it as a metal. *(2 marks)*

   b) State **two** properties of rubidium which are unusual in metals. *(2 marks)*

   c) State **one** other general property of metals which is not shown in the table. *(1 mark)*

Appearance	Silvery-white
Melting point	39°C
Boiling point	688°C
Hardness	Very soft
Ductility	Ductile
Reactivity	Highly reactive

4 The graph below shows the melting and boiling points of the Group 7 elements.

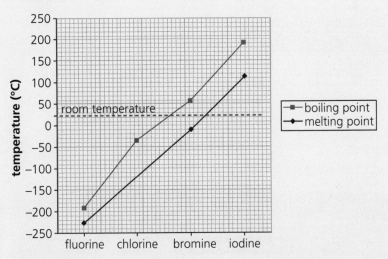

   a) Use the graph to estimate the melting point of chlorine, which is not shown. *(1 mark)*

   b) Which of these elements are gases at room temperature? Explain your answer. *(3 marks)*

Go online for answers

Compounds

Forming compounds

Revised

- Compounds are formed by the **chemical bonding** of two or more different elements.
- When elements react with each other to make a compound, the atoms re-arrange making new bonds.
- During a chemical reaction the total number of atoms present before the reaction equals the total number of atoms after the reaction.

Compounds have their own chemical formula. For example when hydrogen burns with the oxygen in air the compound water is formed:

$$\text{hydrogen} + \text{oxygen} \longrightarrow \text{water}$$

$$2H_2(g) + O_2(g) \longrightarrow 2H_2O(l)$$

During the reaction, two molecules of hydrogen (each containing two atoms) react with one molecule of oxygen (each containing two atoms of oxygen) forming two molecules of water (each containing two atoms of hydrogen and one atom of oxygen).

Carbon also burns in oxygen forming carbon dioxide:

$$\text{carbon} + \text{oxygen} \longrightarrow \text{carbon dioxide}$$

$$C(s) + O_2(g) \longrightarrow CO_2(g)$$

One atom of carbon bonds with the two atoms of oxygen forming one molecule of carbon dioxide.

Chemical equations

Revised

When writing chemical equations it is important to include the physical state symbols for the reactants and the products. The state symbols are written after the chemical formula, inside brackets. Solids have the symbol (s), liquids (l), gases (g) and aqueous solutions (chemicals dissolved in water, like acids) (aq).

Chemical equations tell us:

- the names of the chemical reactants and products
- how many atoms of each element are present in the chemical
- how much of each reactant and product is involved
- the physical state of each reactant and product.

Examiner tip

When drawing space-filler diagrams the exact atom sizes are not important but shading must be unambiguous. The atoms should touch but you only get penalised once if there are small gaps between them.

Examiner tip

When questions state that you should only use the information given, do not use other information to answer the question.

Space-filler diagrams

Space-filler diagrams are used to show the arrangement of atoms in simple molecules. They are a good way of modelling the shape of molecules in a similar way to the 3D plastic molecular modelling kits used in schools.

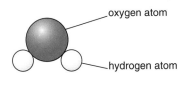
oxygen atom

hydrogen atom

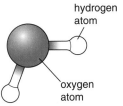
hydrogen atom

oxygen atom

Examiner tip

It is important to study space-filler diagrams very carefully. In the exam, use the key given to write the names or symbols of each atom.

⬆ **Two different models of a water molecule. The one on the left is a space-filler diagram**

Check your understanding

This key represents atoms of some elements.

carbon, C   hydrogen, H   nitrogen, N   oxygen, O

5 a) The gas methane has the formula CH_4. Choose the **letter** of the diagram on the right that represents a molecule of methane.   *(1 mark)*

A   B   C   D

b) **Use the key given above** to draw diagrams representing the molecules:

   i)   hydrogen, H_2 *(1 mark)*

   ii) ammonia, NH_3.   *(1 mark)*

6 The chemical formula of carbonic acid is H_2CO_3.

a) State how many carbon atoms are present in the formula H_2CO_3.   *(1 mark)*

b) Give the **total** number of atoms shown in the formula.   *(1 mark)*

7 The diagrams below represent **six** different substances.

A   B   C   D   E   F

a) Give the letter, A, B, C, D, E or F, of the diagram which represents:

   i) CO_2 *(1 mark)*

   ii) an element   *(1 mark)*

   iii) a compound containing five atoms.   *(1 mark)*

b) Give the chemical formula for substance **D**.   *(1 mark)*

8 The following statements refer to chemical reactions. Which are the **two correct** statements?   *(2 marks)*

   A Atoms are re-arranged during chemical reactions.

   B Some atoms are destroyed in a chemical reaction.

   C Reactants are made during chemical reactions.

   D Reactants are used up during chemical reactions.

Go online for answers

Ionic bonding

The formation of ionic bonds

Revised

When metal atoms react with non-metal atoms, ionic bonds are formed. The metal atoms lose electrons forming positively charged ions, and the non-metal atoms gain the electrons lost by the metal atoms forming negatively charged ions. The oppositely charged ions attract each other forming very strong ionic bonds.

The number of electrons lost or gained by atoms when they form ionic bonds depends on which group of the Periodic Table the element is in. The tables below summarise the ions formed by some of the common elements:

Positive ions	
Name	Formula
Aluminium	Al^{3+}
Calcium	Ca^{2+}
Copper(II)	Cu^{2+}
Hydrogen	H^+
Iron(II)	Fe^{2+}
Iron(III)	Fe^{3+}
Lithium	Li^+
Magnesium	Mg^{2+}
Potassium	K^+
Sodium	Na^+

Negative ions	
Name	Formula
Bromide	Br^-
Chloride	Cl^-
Fluoride	F^-
Iodide	I^-
Oxide	O^{2-}

> **Examiner tip**
>
> A table of common ions will always be published in the back of the examination paper, together with a Periodic Table. Use these to help you to answer questions on this topic.

When ionic compounds are formed, there is no overall charge because the number of positive charges equals the number of negative charges.

Example

Lithium oxide is formed from lithium ions, Li^+, and oxide ions, O^{2-}, when lithium burns in oxygen.

lithium + oxygen $\longrightarrow$ lithium oxide

Two lithium ions are needed to balance the charge on every oxide ion, so the formula of lithium oxide is Li_2O.

Balancing equations

Revised

When balancing chemical equations, the total number of each type of atom has to be the same on each side of the equation. The combustion of lithium in oxygen shows this. Simply putting in the symbols and formulae gives an unbalanced equation:

$Li(s) + O_2(g) \longrightarrow Li_2O(s)$

Oxygen is always found as a diatomic molecule, so there are two oxygen atoms on the left hand side (lhs), but there is only one on the right hand side (rhs). To make this balance we need two lithium oxide 'molecules' on the rhs, but this means there must be four atoms of lithium on the rhs.

To complete the balanced equation we therefore need four atoms of lithium on the lhs. The balanced equation is:

$$4Li(s) + O_2(g) \longrightarrow 2Li_2O(s)$$

Examiner tip

Remember, in a balanced symbol equation the total number of each type of atom must be the same on both sides of the reaction, because atoms cannot be created or destroyed.

Examiner tip

Question **9 a) i)** refers to the ion**s** found in sodium chloride – this means you need to write **both** down.

Check your understanding ———————————— Tested

9 The diagram on the right shows chlorine reacting with sodium.

a) Refer to the tables of common ions (on page 58) to answer these questions.

   i) Give the **formulae** of the **ions** found in sodium chloride. *(1 mark)*

   ii) Give the chemical **formula** for sodium chloride. *(1 mark)*

b) The **word** equation below represents the reaction between sodium and chlorine.

   sodium + chlorine ⟶ sodium chloride

   i) Name the **metal** from the word equation. *(1 mark)*

   ii) Name the **product** of the reaction. *(1 mark)*

— chlorine gas

— white sodium chloride formed on the sides of the gas jar

— burning sodium

10 Refer to the table of common ions to answer this question. The following table shows information about some compounds. Complete the table. *(4 marks)*

Compound	Formula	Metal ion present	Non-metal ion present
sodium chloride	NaCl	Na^+	Cl^-
potassium oxide		K^+	O^{2-}
magnesium bromide	$MgBr_2$		
		Ca^{2+}	I^-

11 Sodium and chlorine are both very reactive elements. When hot sodium is lowered into a gas jar of chlorine, the metal ignites and sodium chloride is formed. Which of the following is the correctly balanced symbol equation representing this reaction?

A $Na + Cl_2 \longrightarrow NaCl$

B $Na + Cl \longrightarrow NaCl$

C $Na + Cl_2 \longrightarrow NaCl_2$

D $2Na + Cl_2 \longrightarrow 2NaCl$

E $2Na + Cl \longrightarrow Na_2Cl$ *(1 mark)*

12 Sodium reacts vigorously with fluorine to give sodium fluoride as shown in the following word equation.

sodium + fluorine ⟶ sodium fluoride

Complete the balanced symbol equation below. *(1 mark)*

_____ Na + _____ $F_2 \longrightarrow$ _____ NaF

Go online for answers ———————————————— Online

Metals and ores

Metals, ores and reactivity Revised

- An ore is a substance found in the Earth's crust containing metal atoms combined with other elements. Examples are hematite and magnetite (iron), and bauxite (aluminium).
- Metals can be extracted from their ores by chemical reactions or electrolysis.
- Some very unreactive metals, like gold, silver and platinum, can be found uncombined with other elements.
- The difficulty of extracting metals from their ores (amount of energy needed) increases as their reactivity increases.
- Metals can be arranged in order of their reactivity in a reactivity series.
- Any metal can displace a metal lower than it in the reactivity series from a solution of one of its salts (e.g. magnesium can displace copper from a solution of copper sulfate, forming magnesium sulfate).

magnesium + copper sulfate $\longrightarrow$ copper + magnesium sulfate

$$Mg(s) + CuSO_4(aq) \longrightarrow Cu(s) + MgSO_4(aq)$$

More reactive	Potassium
	Sodium
	Calcium
	Magnesium
	Aluminium
	Zinc
	Iron
	Tin
	Lead
	Copper
	Silver
Less reactive	Gold

↑ **A reactivity series**

Extracting metals from their ores Revised

Many chemical reactions used to extract metals from their ores involve the processes of reduction and oxidation:

- **Reduction** involves the removal of oxygen atoms from a chemical.
- **Oxidation** involves the addition of oxygen atoms to a chemical.

Extraction of iron

The extraction of iron from iron ore is an example of a reduction/oxidation reaction. In this reaction, iron oxide ore is reduced to iron at high temperatures (in a blast furnace) by the oxidation of carbon (from coke) while carbon (and carbon monoxide), are oxidised to carbon dioxide.

Extraction of aluminium

- Aluminium is higher than iron and carbon in the reactivity series, so we need much more energy to extract it from its ore and reduction/oxidation reactions involving carbon cannot be used.
- Aluminium (and higher metals in the reactivity series) are extracted using **electrolysis.**
- Aluminium oxide is heated to high temperatures making it melt. This allows positively charged aluminium ions to move towards the negatively charged cathode, forming aluminium atoms that can be extracted as bulk aluminium metal.

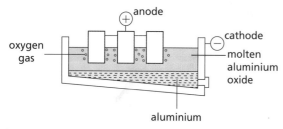

↑ **Electrolysis of aluminium oxide**

Sustainability issues with the extraction of metals from their ores

Revised

● Siting of the plant (large land use, contamination of land) environmental impact, effect on local population

● Fuel and energy costs

● Greenhouse gas emissions

● Impact of recycling

● Effects of the extraction of the ores on the environment and the local population

Examiner tip

Question **13** is quite a complex question with several different parts, lots of text and two diagrams. Read the text carefully and study the diagrams several times before trying to answer the questions.

Examiner tip

The command words **state** and **give** mean that a concise answer is expected without supporting evidence.

Check your understanding

Tested

13 This question is about the reactivity of metals.

a) A teacher carried out the following two experiments in a fume cupboard.

mixture of aluminium and iron oxide

Experiment 1: A mixture of aluminium powder and iron oxide was heated strongly using the equipment shown. The reaction that took place can be summarised by the following word equation:

aluminium + iron oxide ⟶ aluminium oxide + iron

Experiment 2: The experiment was then repeated using a mixture of iron powder and copper oxide. The word equation for this reaction is shown below:

iron + copper oxide ⟶ iron oxide + copper

HEAT

↑ **Experiment 1**

i) Use the results of the two reactions to place the three metals, aluminium, copper and iron, in order of decreasing reactivity. *(2 marks)*

ii) The teacher said that iron oxide, in Experiment 1, and copper oxide, in Experiment 2, had both been 'reduced'. State the meaning of the term reduced. *(1 mark)*

b) Zinc is more reactive than copper. Excess zinc powder was added to blue copper sulfate solution. During the reaction, the blue solution became colourless and a brown solid was formed, as in the diagram.

i) Name the colourless solution, A. *(1 mark)*

ii) Name the brown solid, B. *(1 mark)*

14 Metal **X** is suspected to lie between magnesium and iron in the reactivity series. Describe and explain how you would show this was true using the following chemicals: magnesium ribbon, iron filings and metal **X**, solutions of magnesium nitrate, iron nitrate and the nitrate of metal **X**. *(4 marks)*

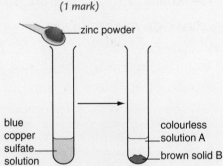

↑ **Zinc powder reacting with copper sulfate solution**

Go online for answers

Online

Properties and uses of metals and nano-scale particles

Properties and uses of some common metals
Revised ☐

Aluminium

● Properties – strong, low density, good conductor of heat and electricity, resistant to corrosion

● Uses – high-voltage power lines, saucepans, window and greenhouse frames, drinks cans, aeroplane and car parts

Copper

● Properties – very good conductor of heat and electricity, malleable, ductile, lustrous, attractive colour

● Uses – in alloys like brass and bronze, water pipes, electrical wires, jewellery and ornaments, saucepan bottoms

Titanium

● Properties – hard, strong, low density, high melting point, resistant to corrosion

● Uses – jet engine and spacecraft parts, industrial machine parts, car parts, medical implants, strengthening steel, jewellery, sports equipment

Alloys
Revised ☐

Alloys are mixtures of two or more different metals (or carbon) made by combining the molten metals. The properties of the alloy can be modified by varying the types and amounts of the metals in the mixture. Examples of common alloys are brass, bronze and stainless steel.

Alloy	Composition	Examples of uses
Brass	Copper and zinc	decorative metal parts low friction metal parts (locks, gears) plumbing and electrical applications musical instruments
Bronze	Copper and tin	boat and ship fittings sculptures and statues guitar and piano strings non-sparking hammers and other tools used in explosive atmospheres
Stainless steel	Iron, carbon and chromium	cookware and cutlery surgical instruments car and spacecraft parts large building and bridge construction jewellery and watches

Nano-particles

- Nano-particles are tiny particles (usually between 1 and 100 nanometres in size – 1 nm = 1×10^{-9} m) that are added in very small quantities to products to give the product a special property.

- Silver is one of the most commonly used nano-particles. It is added to products to make them antibacterial. Products that benefit from this are fridges and other household appliances, soaps, clothes and medical dressings – products that commonly come into contact with human skin.

- Gold nano-particles are used to manufacture high-efficiency solar panels and small but high capacity and voltage batteries.

- There are potential health and environmental questions associated with the use of nano-particles. For example, it is known that in high quantities, metals like silver can be toxic; more research is needed to investigate these claims.

> **Examiner tip**
>
> Words in **bold** in a question are like this for a specific reason. Question **15** says to '**Use the information in the table**'. If you use other information, from memory, you won't get the marks.

Check your understanding

15 The following table shows some examples of different types of steel. **Use the information in the table** to answer the questions that follow.

Name	Composition	Properties
Cast iron	iron, 2–5% carbon	hard but brittle, corrodes easily
Mild steel	iron, 0.1–0.3% carbon	tough, ductile and malleable, good tensile strength, corrodes easily
High carbon steel	iron, 0.7–1.5% carbon	harder than mild steel but more brittle, corrodes easily
Stainless steel	iron and carbon, 16–26% chromium	hard and tough, hardwearing, doesn't corrode

a) Name the **metallic** element that is added to iron to make stainless steel. *(1 mark)*

b) Suggest a reason why cast iron is **more brittle** than mild steel. *(1 mark)*

c) Name the type of steel most suitable for making car bodies. *(1 mark)*

d) Give the main reason why stainless steel is used to make cutlery. *(1 mark)*

16 Nano-sized particles of titanium dioxide are used in sun creams.

a) Give the size range of nano-particles. *(1 mark)*

b) A magazine article contained the following quotes about the use of nano-particles.

Quote 1: *'People are concerned that nano-particles used in cosmetics are not safe.'*

Quote 2: *'There will be no ill effects as larger particles of the same substance are perfectly safe.'*

Give a reason why Quote 2 is considered incorrect by many. *(1 mark)*

c) Explain why some people are concerned about using cosmetic products that contain nano-particles. *(2 marks)*

Go online for answers

Hydrogen and oxygen

Production of non-metals

- Many non-metals are found in the air, including nitrogen (about 78%), oxygen (about 21%) and argon (less than 1%). These gases can be extracted commercially by fractional distillation of liquid air.

- Hydrogen and oxygen can be produced from water by electrolysis and twice as much hydrogen as oxygen is produced.

$$water \longrightarrow hydrogen + oxygen$$
$$2H_2O(l) \longrightarrow 2H_2(g) + O_2(g)$$

Testing for hydrogen and oxygen

- The chemical test for hydrogen gas is to collect the gas and ignite it with a **lighted** splint – hydrogen explodes with a 'squeaky pop'.

- The chemical test for oxygen gas is to collect the gas and insert a **glowing** splint into the test-tube – oxygen will **re-light** the glowing splint.

- Hydrogen burns in air producing energy that can be used as a power source (e.g. as rocket fuel):

$$hydrogen + oxygen \longrightarrow water$$
$$2H_2(g) + O_2(g) \longrightarrow 2H_2O(g)$$

- Hydrogen and oxygen are two of the most important gases that we use.

The uses of oxygen

- In medicine as an aid to breathing
- For producing high temperatures, as in oxyacetylene welding
- In liquid form to burn with rocket fuel

The uses of hydrogen

- In the petrochemicals industry for making certain types of hydrocarbon
- In the food industry for making margarine
- As a fuel in hydrogen fuel cells

Hydrogen is potentially an excellent source of energy – particularly for cars and lorries.

Advantages

- High energy yield
- Non-polluting

Disadvantages

● Highly flammable (explosive)

● Needs to be stored in a pressurised tank

● Few 'filling stations' at present

● Electricity is used to manufacture hydrogen from water by electrolysis – so the whole process is only totally environmentally friendly if the hydrogen is produced by electricity generated from renewable energy sources.

Examiner tip

Remember that with Quality of Written Communication questions like Question **18** part **c)**, the examiners will be looking for clear explanations. If you get the basic facts right but your explanation is not clear or lacks detail, you may lose marks. See pages 110–111 for more help answering QWC questions.

Check your understanding   Tested

17 The pie-chart illustrates the composition of air.

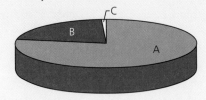

a) State the names of the substances marked
   A, B and C.   *(1 mark)*

b) Name the process by which gases are extracted
   commercially from air.   *(1 mark)*

18 Hydrogen gas is potentially the answer to any future world fuel shortage. Hydrogen is the most abundant element in the Universe and is in plentiful supply on Earth (combined with oxygen in water molecules). Electrolysis can be used to split water molecules to produce hydrogen gas, H_2, and oxygen gas, O_2.

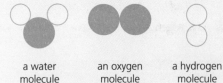

a water molecule   an oxygen molecule   a hydrogen molecule

a) State why electrolysis of water produces twice the amount of
   hydrogen that it does of oxygen.   *(1 mark)*

b) Describe how you would prove that a gas is indeed hydrogen. *(1 mark)*

c) Use the following data to evaluate the potential of hydrogen as a replacement for petrol and diesel to fuel cars. A complete response will include reference to advantages and disadvantages.   *(6 marks QWC)*

Source	water
Extraction method	requires electricity
Amount of energy released on burning	large
Product of burning	water vapour
Ease of ignition	ignites easily
State at room temperature and pressure	gas
Stability	forms explosive mixture with air

Go online for answers   Online

The halogens and the noble gases

What are the halogens and the noble gases?

The **halogens** is the name for the elements in Group 7 of the Periodic Table (fluorine, chlorine, bromine, iodine and astatine).

● The halogens react with metals to produce halides – fluorides, chlorides, bromides and iodides.

● The reactivity of the halogens increases going up the group – fluorine is the most reactive non-metal.

● Chlorine and iodine can be obtained from the compounds produced by the evaporation of sea water (mostly sodium chloride and potassium iodide), but this is no longer considered to be an economical source of iodine.

The **noble gases** is the name for the very unreactive elements in Group 0 of the Periodic Table (helium, neon, argon, krypton and xenon).

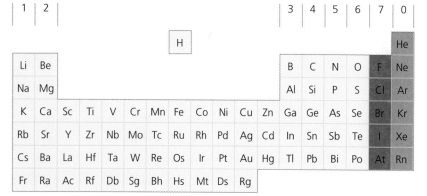

↑ **The position of the halogens (red) and the noble gases (green) in the Periodic Table**

Examiner tip

You can be given quite large tables in an examination question. They might show several patterns and trends. Make sure that you use the correct column of the table – perhaps highlight or put a circle around the correct column in the exam.

Properties and uses

Chlorine (Cl$_2$)

● Pale yellow-green gas
● Poisonous/toxic
● Used to kill bacteria (e.g. in swimming pools)

Iodine (I$_2$)

● Shiny-grey solid or purple gas
● Poisonous/toxic
● Used to kill bacteria (in particular, as a wound dressing)

Helium (He), neon (Ne) and argon (Ar)

● Colourless gases
● Very unreactive
● Helium is used as a filler gas for party balloons and airships
● All three are used in the manufacture of fluorescent tubes (helium glows red, neon orangey-yellow and argon electric-blue)

Fluorine, in the form of sodium fluoride, is added to toothpaste (and drinking water in some areas) to prevent tooth decay.

All scientific and statistical evidence and studies show that adding fluoride to the mains water supply substantially reduces tooth decay. However, some people object to the fluoridation of water as this effectively forces medication upon everyone.

Examiner tip

The addition of sodium fluoride to the water supply is an example of scientific ethics. There may not be 'correct' answers to the questions asked. In this case the examiner is looking for **your** opinions – remember to state your opinion and back it up with an explanation if you can. Sometimes you are asked for reasons 'for' and 'against' something – make sure you give at least one of each.

Check your understanding — Tested

19 Sodium fluoride is added to the water supply in some areas because fluoride ions have been shown to cause a reduction in tooth decay. Scientists established this link by carrying out large-scale surveys.

a) Give a reason why scientists required large numbers of people to complete their surveys in order to establish the link between fluoride ions and a reduction in tooth decay. *(1 mark)*

b) Suggest why it would be better for this type of survey to be carried out by an independent consumer group rather than by a company which manufactures toothpaste. *(1 mark)*

c) Give **one** reason why many people are against the fluoridation of the water supply. *(1 mark)*

20 a) The table below shows some physical properties of the Group 7 elements.

Element	Melting point/°C	Boiling point/°C	Density/ g/cm³	Electrical conductivity	Colour of vapour
Fluorine	−220	−188	1.11	poor	pale yellow
Chlorine	−110	−35	1.56	poor	green
Bromine	−7	59	3.12	poor	brown
Iodine	114	184	4.93	poor	purple

Give the state (**solid, liquid** or **gas**) of:

i) bromine at 60 °C *(1 mark)*

ii) chlorine at −40 °C. *(1 mark)*

b) i) State **one** property of Group 7 elements which shows that they are non-metals. *(1 mark)*

ii) Describe the trend in the melting points of Group 7 elements going down the group. *(1 mark)*

c) State why adding chlorine to the water supply makes the water safe to drink. *(1 mark)*

Go online for answers — Online

Acids and alkalis

pH

Revised ☐

Substances can be classified as acids or alkalis using the pH scale. Acids have a pH lower than 7 and alkalis have a pH higher than 7; pH 7 is neutral. pH is measured using a chemical **indicator** (such as Universal Indicator paper) or an electronic pH meter.

0	1	2	3	4	5	6	7	8	9	10	11	12	13	14
strong acids			weak acids					weak alkalis				strong alkalis		
battery acid, strong hydrofluoric acid	hydrochloric acid secreted by stomach lining	lemon juice, gastric acid (stomach acid), vinegar	grapefruit, orange juice, soda water, wine	tomatoes, acid rain, beer	soft drinking water, black coffee, pure rain	urine, egg yolks, saliva, cows' milk	pure water	sea water	soapy water	Great Salt Lake, milk of magnesia, detergent	ammonia solution, household cleaners	household soda	bleaches, oven cleaner, caustic soda	liquid drain cleaner

increasingly acidic →   increasingly alkaline

⬆ **The pH scale**

Reactions of metals with acids

Revised ☐

Some metals will react with acids. Their reaction depends upon their position in the reactivity series. Metals at the top of the reactivity series react very vigorously and exothermically (explosively) with dilute acids, whereas those metals at the bottom of the reactivity series do not react at all.

Metals react with **acids** forming salts and **hydrogen**.

$$\text{metal + acid} \longrightarrow \text{metal salt + hydrogen}$$

Reactions with hydrochloric acid

Reactions involving hydrochloric acid form salts called chlorides.

$$\text{metal + hydrochloric acid} \longrightarrow \text{metal chloride + hydrogen}$$

For example:

$$\text{magnesium + hydrochloric acid} \longrightarrow \text{magnesium chloride + hydrogen}$$

$$Mg(s) + 2HCl(aq) \longrightarrow MgCl_2(aq) + H_2(g)$$

Reactions with sulfuric acid

Reactions involving sulfuric acid form sulfates.

$$\text{metal + sulfuric acid} \longrightarrow \text{metal sulfate + hydrogen}$$

For example:

$$\text{magnesium + sulfuric acid} \longrightarrow \text{magnesium sulfate + hydrogen}$$

$$Mg(s) + H_2SO_4(aq) \longrightarrow MgSO_4(aq) + H_2(g)$$

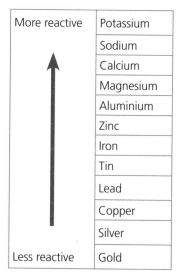

More reactive	Potassium
	Sodium
	Calcium
	Magnesium
	Aluminium
	Zinc
	Iron
	Tin
	Lead
	Copper
	Silver
Less reactive	Gold

⬆ **A reactivity series**

Examiner tip

The charge on the ions is needed to work out the numbers of each ion in the compound. The charges need to balance – equal number of positive and negative charges.

Reactions with nitric acid

Reactions involving nitric acid form nitrates.

metal + nitric acid ⟶ metal nitrate + hydrogen

For example:

magnesium + nitric acid ⟶ magnesium nitrate + hydrogen

$$Mg(s) + 2HNO_3(aq) \longrightarrow Mg(NO_3)_2(aq) + H_2(g)$$

Check your understanding Tested

21 A small piece of magnesium ribbon was placed into excess dilute hydrochloric acid in a boiling tube. The temperature of the reaction mixture was recorded using a temperature sensor and displayed on a computer screen.

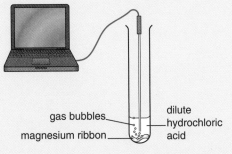

gas bubbles
magnesium ribbon
dilute hydrochloric acid

a) Use the graph to answer parts i) and ii).

   i) State the time taken for the reaction to come to an end. *(1 mark)*

   ii) State the maximum temperature **rise** recorded during the reaction. *(1 mark)*

b) Give **one** advantage of using a temperature sensor and computer to record the temperature. *(1 mark)*

c) i) Other than the temperature change, give **two** observations which suggest that a chemical change is occurring when magnesium is added to dilute acid. *(2 marks)*

   ii) The following table shows the colours of Universal Indicator at different pH ranges. One of the products of the reaction is magnesium chloride. Magnesium chloride solution is neutral. Give the colour of Universal Indicator in magnesium chloride solution. *(1 mark)*

Colour	Red	Orange	Yellow	Green	Blue	Navy blue	Purple
pH range	0–2	3–4	5–6	7	8–9	10–12	13–14

22 Use the table of ions below to write word equations and balanced symbol equations for the following reactions between metals and acids:

a) magnesium and nitric acid *(3 marks)*

b) lithium and hydrochloric acid *(3 marks)*

c) calcium and sulfuric acid. *(3 marks)*

Positive ions		Negative ions	
Lithium	Li^+	Chloride	Cl^-
Calcium	Ca^{2+}	Sulfate	SO_4^{2-}
Magnesium	Mg^{2+}	Nitrate	NO_3^-

Go online for answers Online

Neutralisation

Neutralisation reactions

Revised

- Acids react with metal oxides, metal hydroxides (both called bases) and metal carbonates.

- Soluble bases are called alkalis, such as sodium hydroxide.

- These reactions are all **exothermic**; they give out heat to their surroundings.

- When acids react with bases/alkalis this is called **neutralisation**. For example:

  acid + base ⟶ metal salt + water

  hydrochloric acid + calcium oxide ⟶ calcium chloride + water

  $2HCl(aq)$ + $CaO(s)$ ⟶ $CaCl_2(aq)$ + $H_2O(l)$

  acid + alkali ⟶ metal salt + water

  nitric acid + sodium hydroxide ⟶ sodium nitrate + water

  $HNO_3(aq)$ + $NaOH(aq)$ ⟶ $NaNO_3(aq)$ + $H_2O(l)$

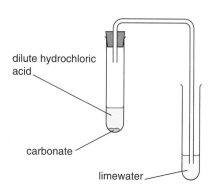

dilute hydrochloric acid

carbonate

limewater

⬆ **Apparatus for the carbonate test**

- Metal **carbonates** react with acids forming metal salts, water and **carbon dioxide** gas. For example:

  acid + metal carbonate ⟶ metal salt + water + carbon dioxide

  sulfuric acid + magnesium carbonate ⟶ magnesium sulfate + water + carbon dioxide

  $H_2SO_4(aq)$ + $MgCO_3(s)$ ⟶ $MgSO_4(aq)$ + $H_2O(l)$ + $CO_2(g)$

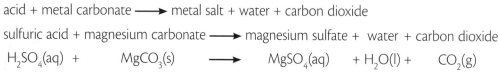

- The chemical test for carbon dioxide gas is to pass it through limewater (calcium hydroxide solution). If the gas is carbon dioxide then the limewater turns 'cloudy' or 'milky'.

- The test for a carbonate is to add an acid. If the substance **effervesces** (gives off bubbles), producing carbon dioxide gas, then it is a carbonate.

Identifying chemicals

Revised

The reactions of an unknown chemical with acids or alkalis and other (known) chemicals can be used as a way of identifying the chemical. This is a common question in the examination. The reactions may be presented in the form of a flow chart and you may have to identify the unknown chemical, **or** you could be given the name of a substance and asked to work out what chemicals react with it in ways that are given in the diagram. In the exam, study the flow chart carefully and use a pencil to write your ideas in and around the diagram – you can always cross or rub them out if you change your mind.

Example

The diagram on page 71 shows some reactions of dilute hydrochloric acid. Give the name for:

1 Metal A: Zinc, because zinc chloride is formed when it is reacted with hydrochloric acid.

2 Gas B: Hydrogen, because reactions of metals with acids produce hydrogen gas.

3 Colourless solution C: Sodium chloride solution, because the reaction of hydrochloric acid with sodium hydroxide produces the salt sodium chloride.

4 Black powder D: Copper oxide, because it reacts with hydrochloric acid producing copper(II) chloride.

> **Examiner tip**
> The style of question in the Example is one commonly used in the exam. You are given a diagram and you have to identify different components from the clues. Practise as many of these questions as you can from the past papers.

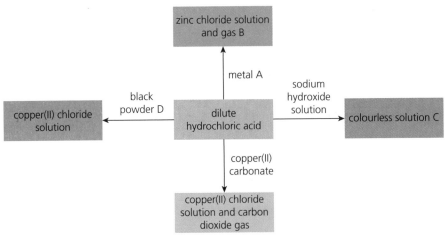

↑ **A flowchart showing some reactions of dilute hydrochloric acid**

Crystals

Revised

● Crystals are large-scale regular arrays (a giant lattice) of a particular solid compound.

● Crystals form as a solution of the compound cools and the solvent (usually water) evaporates.

● Very large crystals can be 'grown' in the laboratory by suspending a seed crystal of the compound into its solution and allowing the solvent to evaporate slowly.

Check your understanding

Tested

23 The diagram below shows the stages in making the compound copper sulfate by reacting copper carbonate with dilute sulfuric acid.

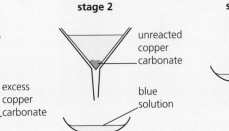

a) State why copper carbonate is added in excess. *(1 mark)*

b) Choose, from the list below, the name for the process occurring in:

  i) stage 2 *(1 mark)*

  ii) stage 3. *(1 mark)*

   boiling   evaporating   dissolving   filtering

c) The reaction that takes place in stage 1 can be described by the following word equation.

   sulfuric acid + copper carbonate ⟶ copper sulfate + water + carbon dioxide

  i) Choose, from the list below, the name of the group of compounds to which copper sulfate belongs. *(1 mark)*

   acid   base   salt

  ii) All of the substances in the above equation are **compounds**. State how compounds are different from elements. *(1 mark)*

d) If sodium carbonate were used instead of copper carbonate, give the chemical name of the crystals formed in the evaporating basin in stage 3. *(1 mark)*

Go online for answers

Online

Crude oil and its uses

Crude oil is a complex mixture of chemicals called **hydrocarbons**. Hydrocarbons are made up of only hydrogen and carbon. Crude oil was formed over millions of years from the remains of simple marine organisms by a process of fossilisation. For this reason, it is called a **fossil fuel**. The components of crude oil can be separated to make many useful chemicals.

Crude oil as a finite resource
Revised

Crude oil is a finite resource. In other words, there is a limited supply of it on the planet. Decisions made about its use have global social, economic and environmental impacts.

● Social impacts – people use the fuels produced from crude oil for heating and transport. If fuel becomes scarce it also becomes expensive and this could have a major impact on people's lives.

● Economic impacts – some countries have oil fields, which means that they can sell fuels to other countries which do not. The countries without oil have no control over the price, and have to pay whatever the oil-producing countries decide to charge.

● Environmental impacts – oil is a pollutant, and produces carbon dioxide when burnt. Oil spills can have serious effects on wildlife and tourism, and the burning of fossil fuels contributes to global warming by adding carbon dioxide to the atmosphere.

Separating crude oil fractions
Revised

The different compounds in crude oil have different boiling points. By heating crude oil and then condensing the vapour at various temperatures, the oil can be separated into less complex mixtures, called fractions. This process is called **fractional distillation**.

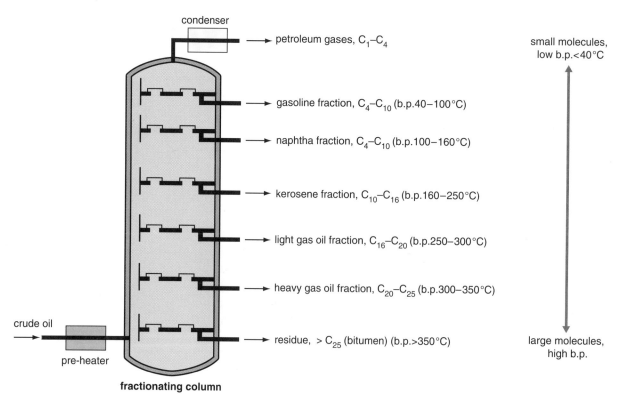

↑ **A fractionating column showing the fractions obtained from crude oil**

www.therevisionbutton.co.uk/myrevisionnotes

The compounds in the crude oil with smaller molecules have lower boiling points and evaporate earlier than the larger molecules when the oil is heated. As they go up the column, they cool and condense, and can be collected.

Notice that the fractions are not pure chemicals but are still mixtures, although the fractions are much simpler mixtures than the original crude oil. Most of the fractions are used as fuels (petrol, diesel, paraffin, etc.) but some are used to make plastics, as we shall see in the next section.

Examiner tip

You will not necessarily have been taught the answers to Question 24 parts **b)** and **c)**. The examiner is trying to find out if you can use your knowledge to solve problems about experimental design. There will always be some questions like this.

Check your understanding ──────────────────────────────── Tested ▢

24 Crude oil can be separated into its fractions using the apparatus shown below.

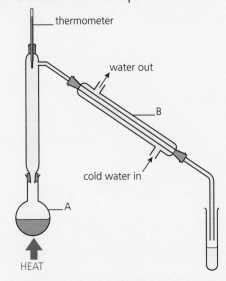

a) Name the physical processes that take place in the parts of the apparatus labelled **A** and **B**. *(2 marks)*

b) State the purpose of the thermometer. *(1 mark)*

c) State the purpose of the cold water. *(1 mark)*

d) Give the name of the overall process taking place. *(1 mark)*

25 Crude oil can be separated into fractions using fractional distillation. The table shows some properties of the first three fractions.

Fraction	Boiling point range	Size of molecules (No. of C atoms)	Colour of fraction	Ease of burning
A	Up to 80 °C	C1 – C6	Colourless	Lights easily and burns with a clean flame
B	80–150 °C	C6 – C11	Yellow	More difficult to light and produces some smoke
C	Over 150 °C	C11 and above	Dark orange	Difficult to ignite and gives smoky flame

State which fraction, **A**, **B** or **C**, would be **most** useful as a fuel, giving a reason for your answer. Use the table to help you answer this question. *(2 marks)*

Go online for answers ──────────────────────────────── Online ▢

Plastics and polymers

Most of the fractions from crude oil are used as fuels, but others are further processed by cracking to make small, reactive molecules called monomers, which can be used to make plastics.

Making plastics
Revised

Plastics are made of molecules known as **polymers**. These are long-chain molecules, made up of many smaller units called **monomers**. The process of joining the monomers together to form polymers is known as **polymerisation**. Below are the key facts about the making of plastics:

- Plastics are made from hydrocarbons called **alkanes**.
- The alkanes come from the **naphtha** or **gas oil** fractions of crude oil.
- The monomers to make plastics are made by heating alkanes **under pressure** or with a **catalyst** (which speeds up the reaction). This process is called **cracking** and produces a small alkene, e.g. ethene.
- The monomers are then polymerised to make the plastic.
- Different monomers form different plastics.

> **Examiner tip**
> There are lots of scientific terms used to describe how plastics are made. You need to know the words in bold.

Polymerisation
Revised

Alkenes have a C=C double bond. They are very reactive and can join together to form polymers, as shown below:

ethene → polythene

In the equation above 'n' means a large number. The double bond has been broken and a bond has formed with an adjacent ethene molecule (to the right). A further ethene molecule (to the left) has also contributed a bond.

This is known as **addition polymerisation**.

Properties of plastics
Revised

All plastics are capable of being moulded or shaped, but different plastics have different properties. These properties determine what the plastic can be used for. Some examples are given in the table on the next page.

> **Examiner tip**
> You are not expected to remember all the properties of all the different types of plastics. However, you are expected to know the general properties of plastics. Often, you will be given the properties and asked to link them to a possible use.

Property	Possible uses	Example
Melts at a high temperature	Dishwasher-safe food containers, hot water pipes	Polypropene, PTFE
Rigid	Drink bottles, margarine tubs, guttering	High-density polythene
Flexible	Food film wrap, bin bags	Low-density polythene
Does not absorb water	Drinking cups and bottles, take-away food trays	Polystyrene, polypropene

Disposing of waste plastic
Revised

Waste plastic can be an environmental problem because it does not break down (it is non-biodegradable). It remains in landfill sites, taking up space that cannot then be used for fresh waste. The manufacture of plastics also requires crude oil, which is a finite resource. These problems can be reduced by re-using or recycling plastic waste. Plastics are recycled in different ways and most have a recycling symbol on them, which identifies the plastic so that it can be recycled in an appropriate way.

Check your understanding
Tested

26 It has been suggested that waste plastics could be recycled and used to manufacture houses cheaply and quickly. Evaluate this potential use of waste plastics. In your answer you should refer to:

- the properties of plastics
- what happens to most plastics once they have been used
- the need to make the best possible use of the Earth's natural resources. *(6 marks QWC)*

27 Cracking is the process that oil companies carry out on large hydrocarbons to form smaller, more useful hydrocarbon molecules.

  a) Ethene is one of the products of the cracking of decane, $C_{10}H_{22}$.

   i) Complete the symbol equation below for the cracking of decane. *(1 mark)*

   $$C_{10}H_{22} \longrightarrow C_2H_4 + \underline{\qquad}$$

   ii) Give **one** of the conditions necessary for cracking to take place. *(1 mark)*

  b) Ethene undergoes addition polymerisation to form polythene. Complete and balance the symbol equation below to show the addition polymerisation of ethene. *(2 marks)*

   ethene

  c) Give the reason why ethene can undergo addition polymerisation. *(1 mark)*

Go online for answers
Online

Plate tectonics

The theory of **plate tectonics** has developed from the theory of **continental drift** suggested by a scientist called **Alfred Wegener** in the early years of the twentieth century. Wegener's ideas were not accepted by many scientists at the time, but later evidence has confirmed that his ideas were correct.

The theory of plate tectonics Revised

The main points of the theory are as follows:

- The Earth's surface is made up of a series of large **plates**, which are in constant motion.
- The movement of the plates is very slow.
- The ocean floors are continually moving, spreading from some plate boundaries, and sinking at others.
- The movement is caused by **convection currents** from deep in the Earth.

Wegener's theory Revised

Wegener based his theory on the following evidence:

- The Earth's continents could be roughly fitted together like a jigsaw.
- There were similarities in rock formations on either side of the Atlantic Ocean.
- Similar fossils were found in lands separated by wide oceans.
- Fossils were found of species that seemed to be in the wrong place (e.g. tropical species in Norway) suggesting that continents had moved through regions with different climates.

Wegener's theory was not accepted at the time because he could not suggest any mechanism that could have actually moved large sections of the Earth's surface.

> **Examiner tip**
>
> Questions that are just about Wegener's theory are rare – they are often combined with questions about earthquakes and volcanoes. To answer questions on this section, you really need to **understand** the evidence – just learning it probably won't be enough.

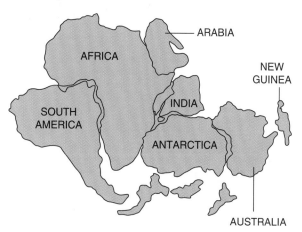

⬆ **An example of how the continents can fit together**

Later evidence

Between Wegener's time and the present day, a number of pieces of evidence have been found that back up Wegener's theory.

- Studies of the ocean floor found large mountain ranges and canyons. If the ocean floor was ancient, it should have been smooth, because of all the sediment coming into it from rivers.

- Samples taken from the floor of the Atlantic Ocean were analysed and dated. This showed that rock in the middle of the Atlantic was considerably younger than that from the eastern or western edges. Rocks could not be dated in Wegener's time.

- The ocean floor was found to be no older than about 175 million years, yet rocks on land had been found that were several billion years old.

- Rocks retain a record of the magnetic field of the Earth, which changes from time to time. Analysis of these magnetic records showed that the continents had moved and gave an idea of where they had moved from and to.

Check your understanding

28 Alfred Wegener proposed the idea of continental drift in 1915. However, other scientists did not accept his idea until the 1960s.

   a) Give **one** piece of evidence that Wegener used to support his idea. *(1 mark)*

   b) Give the main reason why his ideas were not immediately accepted. *(1 mark)*

29 Alfred Wegener's theory of continental drift was rejected by most scientists of his time. Since then, however, new evidence has been found. This includes the following:

'The farther away you travel from a volcanic ridge on the sea floor, the older the crust is, and the older the sediments on top of the crust are.'

   a) Explain how this piece of evidence supports Wegener's theory. *(2 marks)*

   b) What is the name given to the updated theory of continental drift? *(1 mark)*

Go online for answers

Earthquakes and volcanoes

The movement of the Earth's plates against each other results in forces which cause earthquakes and the appearance of volcanoes.

Distribution of earthquakes and volcanoes

Most of the locations of volcanoes and earthquakes lie along lines that mark the boundaries of tectonic plates. Volcanoes occur here because the splits in the crust between two plates are weak points where magma (the molten rock below the Earth's crust) can burst through the crust under pressure.

Volcanoes occur when molten rock (magma) comes through the surface under pressure. Layers of rock cool and set to form the cone of the volcano.

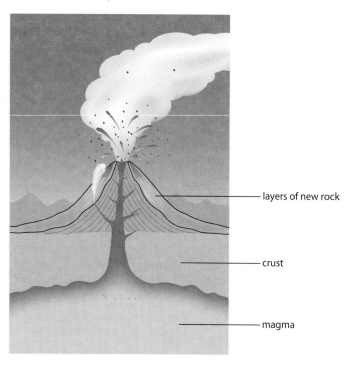

layers of new rock

crust

magma

Earthquakes occur at plate boundaries when plate movement causes a build-up of huge quantities of energy in the rock. This energy is then released, setting up vibrations in the rock.

The fact that most volcanoes and earthquakes occur at plate boundaries helps scientists to predict volcanic eruptions and new earthquakes, but also to work out where the plate boundaries actually are.

Movements at plate boundaries

There are four types of movement at plate boundaries:

- The plates can move apart. Molten rock (magma) below the surface is released. If this happens under pressure, there is a volcanic eruption.
- The plates can collide. This 'crumples' the edges of the plates, forming mountain ranges.
- One plate can slide under the other (this is called **subduction**). Magma is released and volcanoes can occur.
- The plates can slide past one another.

Volcanoes and the atmosphere

Volcanoes played a part in the formation of the Earth's atmosphere, which is discussed in more detail in the next section. The original atmosphere of the Earth was probably composed mainly of **hydrogen** and **helium**, and life as we know it could not survive. At this time, the Earth was still cooling down after its formation. There were large numbers of volcanoes on the surface, constantly erupting. This **outgassing** released a mixture of gases, including **water vapour**, **carbon dioxide** and **ammonia**. The water vapour condensed to form oceans. The gases built up in the atmosphere, and the carbon dioxide also dissolved in the early oceans. Bacteria evolved in the oceans that could use the carbon dioxide to make food, and they gave off **oxygen** as a waste product, adding it to the atmosphere.

> **Examiner tip**
>
> In Question **30** part **b)** you are given the densities of plates A and B. That means you have to use them somewhere in your answer.

30 The Earth's crust (lithosphere) is broken up into huge plates. The diagram shows two plate boundaries A and B.

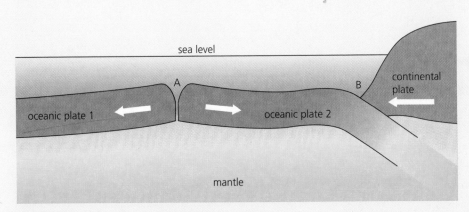

a) Describe what occurs at plate boundary A. *(2 marks)*

b) The two types of plate have different densities as shown in the following table. Describe and explain what occurs at plate boundary B. *(2 marks)*

Type of plate	Density/g/cm³
Continental	2.7
Oceanic	3.0

31 The map on the right shows Mexico. The red dots are volcanoes, and the black dots indicate two cities, Monterrey and Mexico City.

a) Explain the distribution of the volcanoes in and around Mexico. *(2 marks)*

b) Should the citizens of Mexico City or Monterrey be more worried about the possibility of an earthquake? Explain your answer. *(4 marks)*

Go online for answers — Online

Earth's atmosphere

The envelope of gases surrounding the Earth is called its **atmosphere**. The composition of the gases in the atmosphere has changed over time and may change again in the future.

Composition of the atmosphere

Revised

The atmosphere is now made up as follows:

Gas	Percentage/%
Nitrogen	78.1
Oxygen	20.9
Argon	0.9
Carbon dioxide	0.035
Others	0.065

Note that the percentages given are for **dry air**. There is also **water vapour** in the atmosphere, but its percentage varies so it is excluded from the table. The 'other' gases are neon, helium, krypton, hydrogen, xenon, ozone and radon.

How the atmosphere has changed

Revised

The gases in the atmosphere have remained constant for millions of years, although in the last 250 years there has been a significant increase in the level of carbon dioxide. Over the whole history of the planet, the atmosphere has undergone several changes. In effect, the Earth has had three different atmospheres over time.

Atmosphere	Gases	Explanation
1	Hydrogen and helium	Given off as the planet formed. Both gases are light and would have drifted off into space.
2	Carbon dioxide, ammonia and water vapour	Produced as a result of the volcanic activity of the young Earth, which was still cooling down. The water vapour condensed to form oceans.
3	Current composition	Much of the carbon dioxide in Atmosphere 2 would have dissolved in the oceans. Bacteria in the oceans evolved that could use the carbon dioxide and produce oxygen (photosynthesis). The ammonia was converted by sunlight into nitrogen and hydrogen, but the hydrogen drifted into space.

Balance in the atmosphere

Revised

Processes taking place on the Earth can affect the levels of oxygen and carbon dioxide in the atmosphere.

Photosynthesis	Carried out by green plants. It uses up carbon dioxide and produces oxygen.
Respiration	Carried out by all living things. It uses oxygen and produces carbon dioxide.
Combustion	Burning, mainly of fossil fuels. It uses oxygen and produces carbon dioxide.

The effects of photosynthesis and respiration approximately balance each other, but combustion increases the level of carbon dioxide. It has less effect on oxygen levels, because there is much more oxygen than carbon dioxide in the atmosphere. When expressed as a percentage of the atmosphere, a small decrease in oxygen makes little difference. The low level of carbon dioxide in the atmosphere means that a small increase has a larger percentage effect.

Check your understanding

Tested

32 Scientists have been studying the planet Mars and believe that its atmosphere is the same as that which was originally present on the Earth. They have also found that ice exists in craters there. The pie chart shows the composition of the atmosphere on Mars.

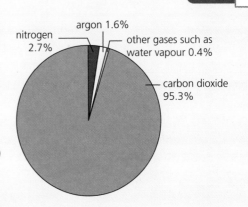

a) Give **two** substances named in the pie chart that were also the main gases present in the Earth's early atmosphere. **(2 marks)**

b) It is believed that the ice in craters on Mars may have been formed from its atmosphere. Explain how this may have happened. **(2 marks)**

33 Global temperature records go back about 160 years, which allows us to draw conclusions about how our climate has changed over this period of time. The graph below shows the average global temperature during the last 160 years.

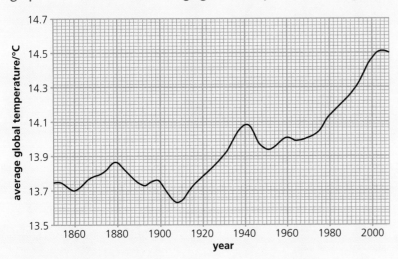

Using the graph:

a) State the average global temperature in 1990. **(1 mark)**

b) Describe the general trend in global temperature since 1910. **(1 mark)**

c) Describe the general trend in global temperature between 1850 and 1910. **(1 mark)**

Go online for answers

Online

Global warming and acid rain

Global warming is one of the major environmental problems facing the world today. It is thought to be caused by the **greenhouse effect**. The nature of the greenhouse effect is covered on pages 100–101. This section deals with the causes and effects rather than the mechanism.

Carbon dioxide and global warming

Revised

Certain gases (but mainly **carbon dioxide**) in the atmosphere act as an insulation around the Earth. During the last 150 years or so, the amount of fossil fuels being burnt has increased enormously because of industrial development. This combustion releases carbon dioxide into the atmosphere, and because of the low levels of the gas in the atmosphere, this has increased the percentage of carbon dioxide in the atmosphere enough for there to have been noticeable effects, and average temperatures on the planet have risen.

Deforestation (felling large numbers of trees which would have absorbed carbon dioxide) has also contributed. Global warming is summarised in the diagram below.

> **Examiner tip**
> Although not everyone agrees that the burning of fuels has caused global warming, the vast majority of scientists accept this as the cause.

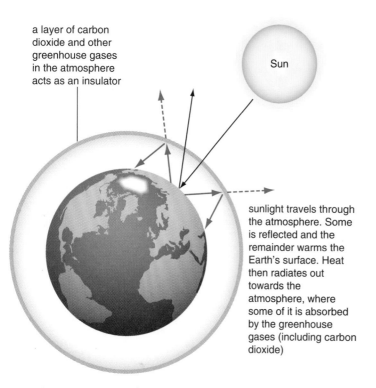

a layer of carbon dioxide and other greenhouse gases in the atmosphere acts as an insulator

Sun

sunlight travels through the atmosphere. Some is reflected and the remainder warms the Earth's surface. Heat then radiates out towards the atmosphere, where some of it is absorbed by the greenhouse gases (including carbon dioxide)

↑ **The principle of global warming**

> **Examiner tip**
> In most of the questions on global warming, data is given about carbon dioxide levels followed by questions about causes and effects.

Disadvantages of global warming

Global warming is a bad thing because:

● Rising temperatures could cause polar ice caps to melt, permanently flooding low-level land around the world.

● Weather patterns could be disrupted, leading to more extreme weather conditions and changes in climate. Some living things would not survive in their changed habitats.

Acid rain

Revised

As well as carbon dioxide, the burning of fuels releases **sulfur dioxide** gas. This is not a greenhouse gas, but it dissolves in the water vapour in the atmosphere to form sulfuric acid, forming **acid rain**. Acid rain is harmful in a number of ways:

● Coniferous trees are particularly sensitive to acids and can be killed by acid rain.

● The acid rain can drain into lakes and rivers, lowering their pH and also releasing aluminium from the soil. Both of these effects kill fish.

● Limestone reacts with acid, so acid rain severely damages limestone buildings and statues.

Carbon capture and sulfur scrubbing

Revised

It is possible to remove some of the harmful gases produced by the burning of fossil fuels before they enter the atmosphere. This is done on a large scale in power plants.

Carbon capture can reduce the carbon dioxide emissions from power stations by around 90%. It is a three-step process:

1   Capturing the CO_2 from power plants and other industrial sources.

2   Transporting it to storage points.

3   Storing it safely in geological sites, such as depleted oil and gas fields.

Post-combustion capture involves capturing the carbon dioxide from the gases given off by burning. A chemical solvent is used to separate carbon dioxide from the waste gases.

There are also techniques being developed for removing the sulfur dioxide from the waste gases produced by power stations. Such processes are referred to as **sulfur scrubbing**, and can reduce the levels of sulfur dioxide by more than 95%.

Check your understanding

Tested

34 The graph shows how levels of carbon dioxide in the air changed between 1750 and the year 2000.

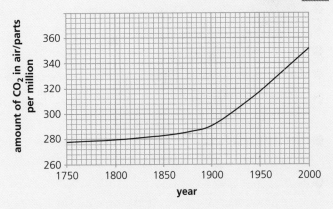

a) Compare the pattern of change shown in the graph before and after 1900.   *(2 marks)*

b) Give **two** possible reasons for the change seen after 1900.   *(2 marks)*

c) State what effect these changes in levels of carbon dioxide are believed to be having on the temperature of the Earth's atmosphere.   *(1 mark)*

d) What is the name given to this effect?   *(1 mark)*

e) Give **one** possible result of this change in the temperature of the Earth's atmosphere.   *(1 mark)*

Go online for answers — Online

Generating electricity from fossil fuels and nuclear power

Generating electricity

Revised

Electricity is the most useful form of energy. Electricity is easy to generate and it easily transforms (changes form) into other useful forms of energy, such as light and heat. Over 90% of the UK's electricity is generated in large power stations using fossil fuels such as coal, oil or gas, or by using nuclear power.

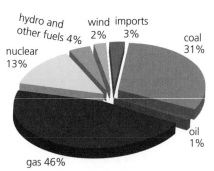

hydro and other fuels 4%
wind 2%
imports 3%
coal 31%
nuclear 13%
oil 1%
gas 46%

↑ **Generation of electricity in the UK by fuel type**

> **Examiner tip**
>
> Always study graphs, diagrams and charts **very** carefully before answering questions based on them.

Advantages and disadvantages of fossil fuels and nuclear power

Revised

The advantages and disadvantages of generating electricity using fossil fuels and nuclear power are:

Advantages

- Cheaper cost of electricity.
- Can be generated on a large scale – large amounts of electricity can be produced in the same location.
- Uninterrupted supply.
- Can be built anywhere (with good access to fuel source – fossil fuels).
- Nuclear power stations do not produce any carbon dioxide when generating the electricity.
- Nuclear power does not produce sulfur dioxide or oxides of nitrogen and so does not contribute to acid rain.
- Nuclear power stations use very small amounts of fuel to produce very large amounts of electricity and only leave small amounts of waste.

Disadvantages

- Very expensive to build.
- The sulfur and nitrogen impurities in fossil fuels produce sulfur dioxide and oxides of nitrogen which make acid rain.
- Coal mining and oil or gas extraction have large effects on the environment.

> **Examiner tip**
>
> Extended writing answers require you to produce written answers where you are careful about the quality of the written communication that you use. Obvious things to check are: spelling, punctuation and grammar, use of key scientific terms and the organisation of your thoughts.

- Large-scale strip-mining of coal produces huge scars on the landscape and the extraction and transportation of oil can produce large amounts of pollution when things go wrong.

- Fossil fuel power stations produce large amounts of carbon dioxide, contributing to the greenhouse effect and global warming.

- Large-scale (fossil fuel) power stations require good rail or sea links to bring large amounts of fuel to the power station. They also need large areas close to the power station to store coal, gas or oil.

- The small amount of waste produced by nuclear power stations is highly radioactive and very dangerous and requires very (expensive) secure storage.

- Nuclear power stations require very expensive and robust safety systems.

Comparing the cost

Cost	Coal power station	Wind farm	Nuclear power station
Commissioning costs: Buying land Professional fees Building costs Labour costs	High	Low	Very high
Running costs: Labour costs Fuel costs	High	Very low	High
Decommissioning costs: Removal of fuel (nuclear) Demolition Clean-up	High	Low	Very high

> **Examiner tip**
>
> **Calculate** means that you must produce a **numerical** answer by doing a mathematical calculation.

Check your understanding
Tested

1. Study the pie chart (on page 84) showing the proportions of electricity generated by different fuels. Calculate the percentage of UK electricity generated from fossil fuels and nuclear power combined. *(1 mark)*

2. Discuss the factors that are involved in making decisions about the type of commercial power station that could be built in an area. *(3 marks)*

3. Large coal-fired power stations are generally built close to lakes or rivers and near to both motorways and mainline railways. Suggest why coal power stations:

   a) require good road and railway links *(1 mark)*

   b) are built near a source of water. *(1 mark)*

4. If you live on the coast of Britain, the area may be ideal for building a power station nearby. The choice may be between having a nuclear or a coal-fired power station built.

   a) People often object to power stations because of their appearance. Write a paragraph describing **three** other objections you could raise to nuclear power stations. *(3 marks)*

   b) Write a paragraph describing **three** objections you could raise, apart from appearance, to coal-fired power stations. *(3 marks)*

Go online for answers
Online

Micro-generation of electricity

What is micro-generation?

Micro-generation of electricity means generating electricity locally on a small scale – very close to where it is needed. Examples of micro-generation are roof-top photovoltaic cells and domestic wind turbines.

Micro-generation has many advantages and some disadvantages over the large-scale generation of electricity from power stations.

Advantages of micro-generation

- Does not produce carbon dioxide and so does not contribute towards the greenhouse effect and global warming
- Does not produce sulfur dioxide or oxides of nitrogen and so does not contribute towards acid rain
- Zero fuel costs
- Higher efficiency of generation
- Can sell some back to National Grid (feed-in)
- Roof-top photovoltaics:
  - Provide 'free' electricity during daylight hours
  - The average system can generate 3 kW of electricity (peak)
- Domestic wind turbines:
  - Provide 'free' electricity when the wind is blowing
  - The average system can generate 6 kW of electricity (peak)
- Micro-water turbines:
  - Provide 'free' electricity from a small stream/river
  - The average system can generate 15 kW of electricity (peak)

Disadvantages of micro-generation

- Erratic energy supply
- Cannot generate large quantities of electricity in one place
- Many locations are very limited in which types of micro-generation can be used
- Some people object to the visual impact of wind turbines and solar panels
- Roof-top photovoltaics:
  - Have a visual impact on roof-tops
  - Need to cover a large area to generate large amounts of electricity
- Domestic wind turbines:
  - Cause a visual impact from the turbine
  - Cause an impact from the noise of the turbine
  - Are unsuitable for most locations – need an un-interrupted, windy site

- Micro-water turbines:
  - Cause a visual impact from the turbine housing
  - Cause an impact from the noise of the turbine
  - Need access to a stream or river

Estimating power output – a wind turbine

Revised

- Area of turbine blades is 25 m²
- Peak wind speed is 12 m/s
- density (of air) = $\dfrac{\text{mass (of air)}}{\text{volume (of air)}}$ = 1.2 kg/m³
- volume of air moving through turbine blades per second = speed × area = 12 × 25 = 300 m³
- mass of air moving through turbine per second = density × volume = 1.2 × 300 = 360 kg
- efficiency of the turbine = $\dfrac{\text{useful power transfer}}{\text{total power input}}$ × 100 = 50 %
- output power of turbine = 6 kW = 6000 W
- input power of wind = 6000 × $\dfrac{100}{50}$ = 12 000 W

Examiner tip

Questions with **more** than one mark require more than one 'fact'.

Examiner tip

Explain means that you must apply some form of reasoning to the recall of theory.

Calculate means that you must produce a **numerical** answer.

Check your understanding

Tested

5   The table shows some of the information planners use to help them decide on the type of power station they will allow to be built.

	Wind	Nuclear
Overall cost of generating electricity (p/kWh)	5.4	2.8
Maximum power output (MW)	3.5	3600
Lifetime (years)	15	50
Waste produced	none	radioactive substances; some remain dangerous for thousands of years
Lifetime carbon footprint (g of CO_2/kWh)	4.64 (onshore) 5.25 (offshore)	5

a) Give **one** reason why the information in the table does not support the idea that wind power will be a cheaper method of producing electricity.   *(1 mark)*

b) Supporters of wind power argue that it will reduce global warming more than nuclear power. Explain whether this is supported by information in the table. *(2 marks)*

c) Supporters of nuclear power argue that it will meet a greater demand for electricity in the future than wind power. Give **two** ways in which this is supported by information in the table.   *(2 marks)*

6   A water turbine is sited in a river flowing at 2 m/s. The density of water is 1000 kg/m³ and 0.15 m³ of water passes through the turbine per second.

a) Calculate the mass of water flowing through the turbine per second.   *(2 marks)*

b) The water turbine produces an electrical output of 48 W. The water inputs 120 W of kinetic energy. Calculate the efficiency of the water turbine.   *(1 mark)*

Go online for answers

Online

The National Grid and transformers

Why do we need a National Grid? ————————————— Revised ☐

Over 90% of the UK's electricity is generated in large-scale power stations. The amount of electricity produced by these power stations is controlled by the National Grid, which provides:

- a reliable, secure energy supply
- an electricity supply that matches the changing demand during the day and over the course of the year
- high voltage power lines that connect all the power stations to the consumers
- electrical substations that control the voltage being supplied to consumers.

The amount of electricity consumed over the course of one day and over the course of the year varies in very predictable ways:

- Peak daily consumption is around six o'clock, when people are cooking evening meals.
- Overall consumption is higher in the winter than in the summer as people use more electricity for lighting and heating.

The National Grid ————————————————————— Revised ☐

When electrical current passes down a wire, it causes the wire to heat up. The heat energy generated from the electricity then transfers into the surroundings, heating the air up around it. The higher the current, the higher the heat loss.

The National Grid is designed to minimise the amount of electrical energy lost as heat as it passes down the power lines. The electricity generated at the power stations is changed by step-up **transformers** to very **high voltages** (typically 400 000 V, 275 000 V or 132 000 V), but very **low current** – so that the energy lost as heat in the power lines is very small (only about 1% of the total energy transmitted).

High voltages would be very dangerous if used in homes and offices, so step-down transformers change the electricity to a lower voltage and higher current for use by consumers.

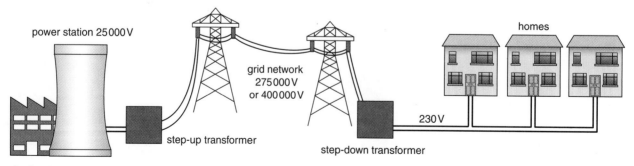

power station 25 000 V · grid network 275 000 V or 400 000 V · homes · step-up transformer · step-down transformer · 230 V

↑ **The National Grid transmission system**

Electrical power

Electrical power is a measure of the rate that electrical energy can be transformed into other more useful forms of energy. Electrical power is calculated using the equation:

electrical power = voltage × current or $P = VI$

In most UK houses, mains voltage V = 230 V.

Example

A mains hairdryer draws a current of 5.5 A. Calculate the power of the hairdryer.

mains voltage = 230 V; hairdryer current = 5.5 A

$P = VI$; power = 230 × 5.5 = 1265 W

Examiner tip

When you are asked to do calculations involving units with prefixes (e.g. kV or MW) make sure that you convert the numbers carefully back into base numbers. 400 kV = 400 000 V and 100 MW = 100 000 000 W.

Examiner tip

Read the instructions to the questions carefully – in Question **7** part **a)** you can use any word from the list **more than once**.

Check your understanding

7 The diagram shows part of the National Grid. Electricity is generated at power station A.

   a) Use the words below to complete the sentences that follow. Each word may be used once, more than once or not at all.

   transformer   pylon   generator   power   current

   i)   At B, a _____ increases the voltage. *(1 mark)*

   ii) Electricity is sent at a high voltage along C, so the _____ is smaller. *(1 mark)*

   iii) At D, the voltage is decreased using a _____. *(1 mark)*

   b) Explain why the electricity is stepped up at B, but stepped down at D. *(3 marks)*

   c) Assume that electricity is transmitted along the cables C at a power of 100 MW and a voltage of 400 kV. Use the equation: power = voltage × current to calculate the current in the cables. *(3 marks)*

8 The diagram shows part of the National Grid.

   a) At which point A, B, C, D or E would you find a step-up transformer? *(1 mark)*

   b) What is the voltage at point C?

   c) Where is the voltage stepped down to 230 V, give the letter A, B, C, D, or E? *(1 mark)*

   d) A high voltage is used in the National Grid so that the electrical energy lost in the cables is: *(1 mark)*

   A zero

   B small

   C big.

Go online for answers

Domestic energy

How do we measure the cost of electricity?

Revised

When you turn on a kettle to boil water to make a cup of tea, the kettle transfers electrical energy into heat energy. The amount of electrical **energy** transferred depends upon the **power** of the kettle and the **time** that the kettle is on.

energy transfer (joules, J) = power (watts, W) × time (seconds, s)

or E = P × t

One joule of electrical energy is a very small amount of energy. A quick-boil kettle can have a power of 3000 W (3 kW), and take about 120 s (2 minutes) to boil a full kettle; this means that the kettle transfers (3000 × 120) = 360 000 J! The joule is therefore an inconvenient unit to use for domestic energy consumption. Instead, we use electrical **units** (measured in kilowatt-hours, kWh). We calculate electrical units using the power (in kilowatts) and the time (in hours).

electrical energy units used = power (in kW) × time (in hours)

We pay for electricity in units. One unit costs around 16p (August 2011), but this price fluctuates from day to day, and depends upon where you live. You calculate the total cost of electricity using the equation:

cost (pence, p) = units used (kWh) × cost per unit (pence, p)

Some typical domestic appliances, their powers (in kW), average time on per day (in hours), number of units used and cost (in pence) are shown in the table below:

> **Examiner tip**
>
> A list of the equations that you will need for each examination paper will be printed inside the front cover of the paper. The question will usually refer you to this list. You need to pick the correct equation from the list. In a three-mark question, you usually get one mark for your choice of equation and two marks for doing the calculation correctly.

Domestic appliance	Power (kW)	Average total time on per day (hours)	Total number of electrical units (kWh)	Total cost per day (p)
Kettle	3.0	0.13	0.39	6.24
Washing machine	0.7	1.5	1.05	16.8
Electric shower	8.5	0.5	4.25	68.0
Desktop computer	0.2	3.0	0.60	9.6
Fridge-freezer	0.04	24.0	0.96	15.36
TV	0.05	4.0	0.20	3.2

The cost of fuel

Revised

There are many different ways to supply energy to a house. Each type of energy supply has its own cost. Remember, the cost of energy varies over the course of the year and also varies due to the state of the world energy market. Typical costs are shown in the table below.

Energy source	Cost per unit (kWh) (p)
Electricity	16
LPG (liquid propane gas)	8
Heating oil	6
Natural gas	5
Smokeless coal	7

The average UK household consumes 16 500 kWh of gas and 3300 kWh of electricity annually. So the average UK cost of energy is (16 500 × 5) + (3300 × 16) = £1353 per annum. This is **not** the cost that the average UK household pays for energy, because it does not include a standing charge that each energy supply company will add to the cost of the energy to take into account its services, etc.

Households can reduce their energy bills by generating their own energy, typically by using roof-top solar panels or small wind turbines (if suitable). The economics of the two main domestic energy generation types are shown in the table below.

Type of energy generation	Power (kW)	Typical cost (£)	Savings per year (£)	Payback time (years)
Solar electricity	2.7	12 000	1100	10.9
Wind turbine (on mast)	6	20 000	3200	6.25

$$\text{payback time} = \frac{\text{cost to buy}}{\text{savings per year}}$$

Examiner tip

Always check your calculations in an examination to make sure that you have not made a mistake, such as inputting the wrong numbers into your calculator!

Check your understanding
Tested

9 A £1 coin, inserted into a pre-payment electric meter, buys 5 units (kWh) of electricity.

a) Use the equation cost of 1 unit = $\dfrac{\text{cost}}{\text{number of units}}$ to calculate the cost of 1 unit. *(1 mark)*

b) Use the equation time (h) = $\dfrac{\text{number of units}}{\text{power (kW)}}$ to calculate how long a 2 kW electric fire can be used before the £1 coin runs out. *(2 marks)*

10 A householder buys gas for heating and cooking, and electricity for lighting and operating electrical appliances. The table shows information about the householder's energy consumption and the total yearly cost.

Year	Units of electricity (kWh)	Units of gas (kWh)	Total units of energy (kWh)	Total cost (£)
1st Jan – 31st Dec 2005	4309	36 958	41 267	866.62
1st Jan – 31st Dec 2006	4540	33 446	37 986	949.65

a) Write down a suitable equation and use it together with data from the table to find the overall cost of 1 unit (kWh) of energy in 2006. *(3 marks)*

b) On 1st January 2006 the householder fitted a solar panel, at a cost of £2000, to provide hot water for heating.

i) Use data from the table to estimate the number of units produced by the solar panel in 2006. *(1 mark)*

ii) Use the answer from part a) to calculate the amount of money saved on his 2006 gas bill. *(1 mark)*

iii) Calculate the time it would take for his annual savings to pay back the cost of the solar panel. *(2 marks)*

iv) Give a reason why the payback time calculated in iii) could be much smaller. *(1 mark)*

Go online for answers
Online

Energy transfer and efficiency

Sankey diagrams

The transfer of energy (or power) from one form to other forms can be shown using a Sankey diagram, which shows not only the types of energy as they transform into different forms but also the amounts involved. The Sankey diagram for an energy-efficient light bulb is shown below.

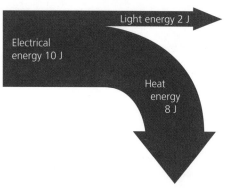

Light energy 2 J

Electrical energy 10 J

Heat energy 8 J

↑ **Sankey diagram for an energy-efficient light bulb**

Sankey diagrams are drawn **to scale** – the width of the arrow at any point shows the amount of energy being transformed. Conventionally, we usually write the type of energy and the amount of energy (or power) on the arrow, and the useful forms of energy usually go along the top of the diagram, with the wasted forms curving off downwards. Sankey diagrams give us not only a good way of showing energy (and power) transfers by a device or during a process, they also show how efficient the process is – the bigger the useful energy arrow is compared to the input arrow, the higher the efficiency.

Efficiency

Efficiency is a measure of how much useful energy (or power) comes out of a device or process compared to the total amount of energy (or power) that goes into the device or process. Efficiency is usually expressed as a percentage using the equation:

$$\% \text{ efficiency} = \frac{\text{useful energy (or power) transfer}}{\text{total energy (or power) input}} \times 100$$

Example

The efficiency of the energy-efficient light bulb can be calculated using data from the Sankey diagram. The total energy input (as electricity) is 10 J. The useful energy output (as light) is 2 J.

$$\% \text{ efficiency} = \frac{\text{useful energy transfer}}{\text{total energy input}} \times 100$$

$$= \frac{2}{10} \times 100 = 20\%$$

> **Examiner tip**
>
> Foundation-tier students are not required to re-arrange equations – but you might have to change numbers given in prefixes, such as kW, back into base units, such as W.

Why is energy efficiency important?

Energy-efficient devices are very important for the future. The more efficient a device is, the more of the energy input is output as useful energy and less is wasted. Conventional fossil-fuel power stations are at best only 33 % efficient. This means that for every 100 tonnes of coal or oil used, only about 33 tonnes is converted directly into useful electricity. The rest of the coal or oil is effectively heating up the atmosphere and producing unnecessary carbon dioxide gas! Wind turbines are about 50 % efficient and solar panels about 30 % efficient.

Standard tungsten filament light bulbs are typically only 2–3 % efficient; 'low-energy' bulbs are about 20 % efficient but LED light bulbs can be up to 90 % efficient. Imagine the effect on electricity consumption if every light bulb in the UK was replaced by an LED bulb!

Examiner tip

There are two types of equation-based questions used in the examination. **Either** you will be given an equation and you need to extract the correct data to use in the equation; **or** you will be given the correct data and you will be asked to select the correct equation from the list at the front of the examination paper.

On the higher-tier paper, you may also need to re-arrange the equation as part of the question.

Check your understanding

11 Water can be boiled using a saucepan on a gas-cooker ring. The energy transfers are shown on the right.

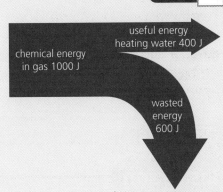

a) Write down an equation and use it to find the efficiency of heating water in this way. *(3 marks)*

b) An electric kettle is 90 % efficient at boiling water. Complete the energy transfer diagram below. The diagram is not to scale. *(2 marks)*

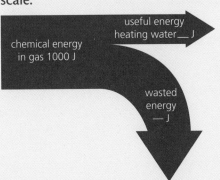

12 The table shows how energy is used in a coal-burning power station. Write down in words a suitable equation and use it to calculate the efficiency of the power station. *(3 marks)*

Energy input per second	Energy output per second
6000 MJ	3350 MJ of energy taken away as heat in the water used for cooling
	2100 MJ of energy fed into the National Grid
	550 MJ of energy given out in the gases released during burning

Home heating

Convection, conduction and radiation

Revised ☐

Homes are heated by transforming energy sources such as electricity or gas into heat using appliances such as electric fires or hot-water radiators. Thermal (heat) energy will move from somewhere **hot** (where the temperature is higher) to somewhere **cold** (where the temperature is lower). It does this by **conduction**, **convection** or **radiation**.

Conduction

Conduction occurs through solids and liquids. Materials such as metals are very good thermal conductors. Materials that do not conduct thermal energy very well are called insulators – many non-metals are good insulators.

Convection

Convection occurs through liquids and gases. When a gas (or liquid) is heated, the particles move faster. As the particles speed up they get further apart, increasing the volume of the gas. This causes the density of the gas to decrease. Less dense gas will float (or rise) above more dense gas. As the gas rises it cools again, the particles slow down, get closer together, increase in density and fall. This creates a convection current which heats the room. Temperature differences within the Earth's mantle and within the atmosphere cause natural convection currents.

Radiation

Thermal radiation is emitted by **hot** objects. A hot-water radiator emits **infrared** electromagnetic radiation. Dull, black objects are good emitters and absorbers of thermal radiation. Shiny, light-coloured objects are good reflectors of thermal radiation. All objects emit thermal radiation, but the higher the temperature of the object the greater the amount of thermal radiation emitted.

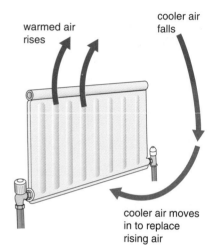

warmed air rises

cooler air falls

cooler air moves in to replace rising air

⬆ **Convection currents transfer heat from the radiator to the room**

Insulation

Revised ☐

The amount of thermal energy escaping from a house can be reduced by using domestic **insulation systems** that work by reducing the effects of thermal conduction, convection and radiation. The table on the next page summarises the main systems that can be installed.

Examiner tip

Home heating questions are classic examples of questions involving the use of data. Question **13** shows information displayed in a table, and Question **14** shows data displayed graphically. In both cases you need to extract information from the data in order to answer the questions. Study the information given carefully, checking column headings, units, graph axes, trends in the data and any labels or annotations.

Insulation system	How it works	Typical installation costs	Typical annual savings	Payback time (years)
Draught proofing	Draught excluders and draught-proofing strips are fitted, reducing the **convection** of hot air through gaps under doors and in window frames.	£50	£50	1
Cavity-wall insulation	Fills the space between the double walls of bricks with foam. The foam traps air, which is a **poor conductor** and prevents air from circulating within the cavity, reducing thermal loss by **convection**.	£250	£110	2.3
Floor insulation	Mineral wool is laid between the joists under the floorboards and silicone sealant is used to seal gaps between skirting boards and floorboards. This reduces thermal loss via conduction and convection.	£140	£70	2
Loft insulation	Mineral wool insulation is laid between the timber joists in the loft. This reduces thermal loss via conduction and convection.	£250	£150	1.7
Double glazing	Two sheets of glass with a gap between them. Reduces thermal loss via conduction and convection.	£2000	£130	15.4

Check your understanding

Tested

13 A homeowner decided to reduce their heating bill by improving their house insulation. The table shows the cost of the improvements made and the yearly savings.

Insulation method	Cost	Yearly saving
Draught-proofing doors and windows	£80	£30
Fitting a jacket to the hot-water tank	£20	£20
Cavity-wall insulation	£1100	£50
Loft insulation	£400	i)
Total	ii)	**£200**

a) Complete the table. *(2 marks)*

b) The homeowner spent £1200 per year heating his house before insulating it. How much would he expect to spend each year after the improvements? *(1 mark)*

c) Give a reason why heat loss by convection is reduced by cavity-wall insulation. *(1 mark)*

14 a) State how double glazing reduces the heat lost through the windows of a house. *(2 marks)*

b) The graph shows the results of an investigation to see how the rate of loss of energy through a double glazed window was affected by the width of the air gap between the two panes of glass. The investigation used a window of area 1 m² and kept a temperature difference of 20 °C between the inside and the outside.

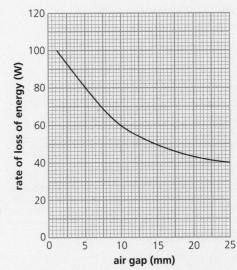

i) Use the graph to estimate the rate of loss of energy for an air gap of 0 mm, and explain how you obtained your answer. *(2 marks)*

ii) Give **two** reasons why most manufacturers of double glazed windows are unlikely to use an air gap any larger than 20 mm. *(2 marks)*

Go online for answers

Online

Describing waves

How do we describe waves?

Revised

Waves are described in terms of their **wavelength**, **frequency**, **speed** and **amplitude**. The diagram shows these quantities on a transverse wave like a water wave, or light, where the direction of vibration of the wave is at right angles to the direction of travel of the wave.

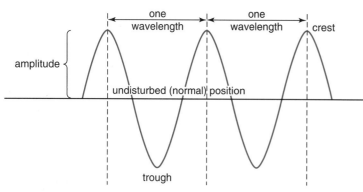

↑ **Wave measurements**

- The **amplitude** of a wave is a measure of the energy carried by the wave. Amplitude is measured from the undisturbed (normal) position to the top of a crest, or the bottom of a trough. Loud sounds will have higher amplitudes than quiet sounds.
- The **wavelength**, λ, of a wave is the distance that the wave takes to repeat itself – this is normally measured from one crest to the next crest. Wavelength is measured in metres, m.
- The **frequency**, f, of a wave is the number of waves that pass a point in 1 second. Frequency is measured in hertz, Hz, where 1 Hz = 1 wave per second.
- The **speed** of a wave, c, is the distance that a wave travels in 1 second. Wave speed is measured in metres per second, m/s.

Calculating speed, frequency and wavelength

Revised

- Wave speed can be calculated using the equation:

$$\text{wave speed} = \frac{\text{distance}}{\text{time}}$$

- Wave speed, frequency and wavelength are all related by the basic wave equation:

$$\text{wave speed} = \text{frequency} \times \text{wavelength}$$

$$\text{or } c = f\lambda$$

- Waves travel at a range of different speeds.
- All electromagnetic waves travel at the speed of light, $c = 300\,000\,000$ m/s or 3×10^8 m/s.
- Water waves, like surf, travel at about 4 m/s.

> **Examiner tip**
>
> Study questions involving diagrams carefully. Question **16** is asking you to measure some quantities from the diagram – you need to revise what the quantities are, before you make measurements from the diagram.

Examples

1. A surfer takes 10 s to travel 50 m on the crest of a wave onto a beach. What is his speed?

$$\text{wave speed} = \frac{\text{distance}}{\text{time}} = \frac{50}{10} = 5 \text{ m/s}$$

2 The wavelength of the waves is 40 m. What is the frequency of the waves?

wave speed = frequency × wavelength; $c = f\lambda$

re-arranged: $f = \dfrac{c}{\lambda} = \dfrac{5}{40} = 0.125$ Hz

3 Calculate the speed of sound waves travelling through wood with a frequency of 5 kHz and a wavelength of 79.2 cm.

First change the units: 5 kHz = 5000 Hz and 79.2 cm = 0.792 m

Then use the equation: wave speed = frequency × wavelength

$c = f\lambda = 5000 \times 0.792 = 3960$ m/s

Examiner tip

In Question **15** you need to use the graph to extract data that you can then input into the equations given. Draw vertical lines on the graph at the required wavelengths and then use horizontal lines across the graph where they hit the curve to find corresponding frequencies.

Check your understanding

Tested

15 The graph shows how the frequency of deep ocean waves depends upon the wavelength of the waves.

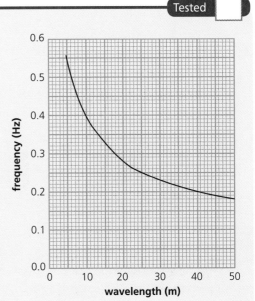

a) Use information from the graph and the equation wave speed = wavelength × frequency to calculate the speed of waves with a wavelength of 40 m. *(2 marks)*

b) A large meteorite falls into the ocean and produces waves with a range of wavelengths.

   i) Use the equation speed = $\dfrac{\text{distance}}{\text{time}}$ to calculate how long it would take 40 m wavelength waves to arrive at an island 5600 m away. *(1 mark)*

   ii) Would 10 m waves arrive before or after the 40 m waves? Use information from the graph to explain your answer. *(2 marks)*

16 The diagram shows a train of waves.

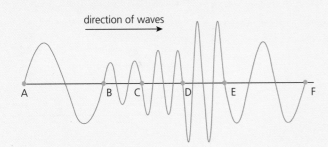

a) How many waves are shown between A and C? *(1 mark)*

b) Between which two of the points, A–F, is:

   i) the wavelength biggest? *(1 mark)*

   ii) the amplitude smallest? *(1 mark)*

c) The eight waves between A and F cover a distance of 240 cm. Calculate the average wavelength of the waves. *(1 mark)*

17 Yellow light travels to us from the Sun at a speed of 3×10^8 m/s. It has a frequency of 5×10^{14} Hz. Write down in words a suitable equation and use it to calculate the wavelength of this yellow light. *(3 marks)*

Go online for answers

Online

The electromagnetic spectrum

What is the electromagnetic spectrum?

The electromagnetic spectrum is a family of (transverse) waves that all travel at the same speed in a vacuum, 300 000 000 m/s or 3×10^8 m/s.

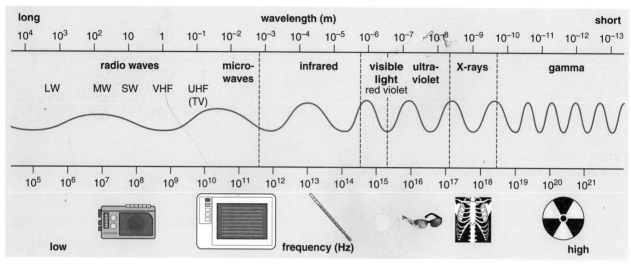

↑ **The electromagnetic spectrum**

The different parts of the electromagnetic spectrum have different wavelengths and frequencies, and energies. The higher the frequency of the wave, the higher its energy. The frequency, wavelength and energy of an electromagnetic wave completely determine its properties and how it will behave.

- **Gamma rays** have very high energy and can ionise (kill or damage) cancer cells, but they are also used to image the body.

- **X-rays** are also ionising, and are also used in medical imaging.

- **Ultraviolet** light can ionise skin cells causing sun-burn.

- **Infrared** radiation is used for heating and communications, such as in remote controls and optic fibres.

- **Microwaves** are also used for heating and communicating, particularly as mobile phone signals. There are some public concerns about possible health risks associated with the microwaves used to transmit mobile phone signals, and in particular, the long-term exposure to low levels of microwaves of children.

- **Radio waves** are used for communications over much longer distances, transmitting TV and radio programmes.

All parts of the electromagnetic spectrum can carry information and energy. Stars also emit all parts of the spectrum giving us information about their composition and behaviour.

> ### Examiner tip
>
> Your answers to questions on this topic rely on your ability to learn the electromagnetic spectrum in order. Commit it to memory – put a large A3 copy of it on the wall of your bedroom – over time you will learn it without even realising it! You could also try to remember it by writing it down several times over the course of a week or month.

All objects emit electromagnetic radiation. Very cold objects are emitting very little radiation.

But as the temperature of the object increases so does the amount of radiation emitted and the frequency of the emitted waves as well.

We recognise this emitted radiation as heat energy when the emitted waves become infrared, but extremely hot objects like stars are emitting all parts of the spectrum in different amounts depending on the star's temperature, mass, composition and stage in its life cycle. The characteristic emission spectrum of a hot object is often called its 'blackbody' radiation curve, shown in the diagram.

You can see from the diagram that as the temperature of the object changes, so does its characteristic blackbody radiation curve, becoming broader (emitting more wavelengths) and emitting waves with a higher intensity.

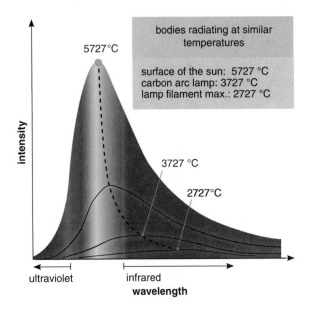

bodies radiating at similar temperatures

surface of the sun: 5727 °C
carbon arc lamp: 3727 °C
lamp filament max.: 2727 °C

↑ Blackbody radiation curves

Check your understanding — Tested

18 a) Using the words below fill in the missing parts of the electromagnetic spectrum. *(2 marks)*

ultraviolet **radio waves** **sound waves** **water waves**

i)	microwaves	infrared	visible light	(ii)	X-rays	gamma rays

b) Some electromagnetic waves can be used for communications.

   i) Name the wave that is used by remote controls. *(1 mark)*

   ii) Name the wave that is used to communicate with satellites in space. *(1 mark)*

c) Some of these waves can be harmful.

   i) Name **one** wave from the list that can ionise cells in the body. *(1 mark)*

   ii) What is the danger from a large dose of infrared rays? *(1 mark)*

19 Study the diagram showing the blackbody radiation curve above. The dotted line shows how the position of the maximum of the graph changes with different temperatures.

a) What is the difference in temperature between a lamp filament and a carbon arc lamp? *(1 mark)*

b) How does the position of the maximum change between the temperature of a lamp filament and a carbon arc lamp? *(2 marks)*

c) How would you describe the emission spectrum of the surface of the Sun? *(3 marks)*

Go online for answers — Online

The greenhouse effect

What is the greenhouse effect?

Why is it that the temperature inside a greenhouse on a sunny day is substantially higher than outside the greenhouse? How is this linked to global warming?

The visible surface of the Sun (called the photosphere) acts like a blackbody radiator (see pages 98–99), emitting peak intensity radiation in the visible part of the electromagnetic spectrum.

The visible light from the Sun passes through our atmosphere, in a similar way to light passing through the glass in the greenhouse. Some of the visible light is absorbed by the atmosphere, but the vast majority of it hits the surface of the Earth – like the ground inside a greenhouse. Much of this visible light is reflected back into space off the surface of the oceans, but some is absorbed by the land.

The absorbed visible light is then re-emitted by the land back up into the atmosphere, but at a much longer wavelength – as infrared radiation.

Some of the longer wavelength infrared radiation is reflected back to Earth by the layer of carbon dioxide and other greenhouse gases like methane and water vapour in our atmosphere – like sunlight reflected by the glass in the greenhouse.

visible energy from the Sun passes through the glass and heats the ground

infrared heat energy from the ground is partly reflected by the glass, and some is trapped inside the greenhouse

↑ **The greenhouse effect**

How is the greenhouse effect related to global warming?

The overall consequence of the greenhouse effect is that more and more of the Sun's energy is being absorbed by the Earth and its atmosphere – causing an overall increase in the Earth's temperature – global warming!

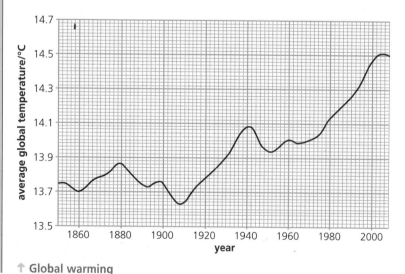

↑ **Global warming**

> **Examiner tip**
>
> If you think that you need to draw a diagram to help you answer a question then do so – even a small diagram in the margin of the paper can help. If the examiner is expecting you to draw a diagram, the question paper will say so and there will be a suitable space for you to draw it.

There have always been periods of global warming (followed by global cooling – ice ages) in the Earth's history. There is a very close correlation between the amount of carbon dioxide in the atmosphere and the average global temperature. **However**, the level of greenhouse gases in the atmosphere has risen dramatically over the past 100 years or so, since the start of the Industrial Revolution, and has risen particularly quickly over the past few decades. The levels of carbon dioxide in the atmosphere are rising due to human activities such as:

● the burning of fossil fuels in power stations to produce electricity, which has increased rapidly

● the use of cars, vans and lorries that burn petrol and diesel as fuels has also increased

● the destruction of vast areas of tropical rainforest for logging and to produce agricultural land.

Check your understanding

Tested

Read the following article about the Eden Project in Cornwall.

The Eden Project in Cornwall is the home of some of the largest and certainly the most spectacular greenhouses (called biomes) in the world. The largest of the greenhouses contains tropical plants and has an average temperature of 24 °C.

The temperature is controlled by a variety of different means, but very little external energy is needed to keep the temperature high. This is because, like all greenhouses, the biomes let radiation from the Sun in but they don't let it escape very easily. As a result,

greenhouses always seem hotter than their surroundings – hence the name 'greenhouse effect'.

Unlike in traditional greenhouses, the biomes at the Eden Project are made of transparent plastic, which acts in a very similar way to our atmosphere.

The conditions inside the tropical biome are changed even more by the water-mist sprayers that are constantly increasing the humidity inside the biome to replicate the conditions in a tropical rainforest.

20 What is the difference between the radiation absorbed by the ground in the biome and the radiation that it emits? *(2 marks)*

21 Why is some of the radiation emitted by the ground in the biome reflected back into the biome? *(1 mark)*

22 **a)** In the greenhouse model of global warming which bit of the biome is like the atmosphere? *(1 mark)*

b) In what ways is the Earth's atmosphere different? *(1 mark)*

23 Explain why the water-misters in the tropical biome at the Eden Project would increase the greenhouse effect inside the biome. *(2 marks)*

24 Explain, with reasons, **three** consequences of global warming via the greenhouse effect. *(6 marks QWC)*

Go online for answers

Online

Communications

Our modern societies have become accustomed to instant communications. You can take out your mobile phone and call someone in Australia from wherever you are in the UK. BBC news correspondents can report live on the news from across the globe via a complex network of satellites and optical fibre links.

Satellite communication

Revised

Satellite communications work using microwaves. Communications satellites are put up into geosynchronous orbit. This means that the satellite takes 24 hours to complete its orbit – the same time as the Earth takes to rotate on its axis – meaning that from the Earth, the satellite appears to be stationary. Microwave signals are sent from an Earth Station dish, like those at BT's Communications Centres at Goonhilly in Cornwall and Madley in Herefordshire. The microwave signal is detected by the satellite and then re-emitted by another dish on the satellite back towards the Earth.

> **Examiner tip**
>
> Be careful with questions on this topic – don't get confused between satellite communications (that use microwaves) and terrestrial TV and radio (that use radio waves).

Optical fibres

Revised

Optical fibre links work by sending phone signals via infrared waves along optical fibres. The infrared waves reflect off the inside surfaces of the fibre. In order for optical fibres to work across the globe, long cables made up of thousands of tiny strands of glass-fibre have been laid across continents and under the oceans – connecting up the world!

Optic fibre communications are much quicker than satellite communications, but both systems introduce a time-delay into the signals.

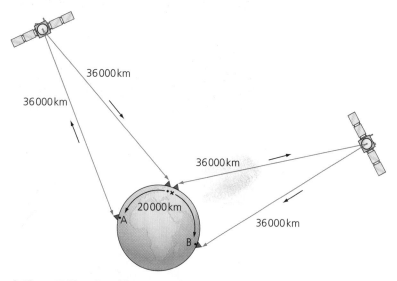

↑ **The satellite signal has much further to travel than the optical fibres**

> **Examiner tip**
>
> Make sure that you bring a ruler to the examination – examiners are expecting to see signal paths drawn as straight lines!

Mobile phones

Mobile phones work by transmitting low power microwave signals to a local base station mast. All base stations are connected to a Mobile Telephone Switching Office (MTSO) and these communicate with each other via optical fibre connections. The mobile phone system constantly keeps track of where each mobile phone is – and the signal is sent to its nearest base station which then sends out another microwave signal to the recipient phone.

Signals sent via optical fibre have advantages over traditional telephone signals sent via wire because:

● Fibre optic lines use less energy.

● They need fewer boosters.

● There is no cross-talk (interference) with adjoining cables.

● They are difficult to bug.

● Their weight is lower so they are easier to install.

Examiner tip

Question **27** is a higher-tier question as it involves re-arranging an equation and the use of standard form. Make sure that you always check calculations on your calculator to ensure that you have put the numbers in correctly.

25 A geosynchronous (geostationary) satellite is used to send signals from A to B.

    a) How long does it take this satellite to orbit the Earth once? *(1 mark)*

    b) **Add to the diagram** to show how **A** sends signals to **B** via the satellite. *(1 mark)*

    c) Name the electromagnetic wave that is used to send signals to satellites. *(1 mark)*

26 Electromagnetic waves are used in communications to send television (TV) signals.

    a) Which part of the spectrum carries TV signals via satellites. *(1 mark)*

    b) Which part of the spectrum carries TV signals from transmitters to an aerial. *(1 mark)*

    c) Which part of the spectrum carries TV signals through optical fibre cables. *(1 mark)*

27 This question concerns long-distance communications between two points on the Earth's surface, A and B, using satellite and optical fibre links.

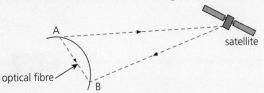

    a) Information is passed from A to B using a satellite in geosynchronous orbit 3.6×10^4 km above the Earth's surface. Microwaves carry the information at a speed of 3×10^8 m/s from A to B via the satellite. Write down an appropriate equation and use it to calculate the time delay between sending and receiving the information. *(4 marks)*

    b) i) The information could also be sent from A to B via a transcontinental optical fibre linking A and B. An infrared signal carries the information at a speed of 2×10^8 m/s. Give a reason why the time delay between sending and receiving this signal is much shorter than that calculated in part **a**). *(1 mark)*

       ii) State **two** other advantages of using optical fibres to send information over long distances. *(2 marks)*

Go online for answers — Online

Ionising radiation

What is radiation?

Radiation is the general term used to describe the emission of electromagnetic spectrum waves and the energy given out by radioactive materials.

Ionising radiation is the term given to the short-wavelength parts of the electromagnetic spectrum (ultraviolet, X-ray and gamma ray) and radioactive emissions of alpha (α), beta (β) and gamma (γ) radiation. These types of radiation have such **high energy** that they can cause atoms to become charged (ionised) by removing electrons. If this occurs inside living cells, the cells can mutate (and possibly cause cancer) or die.

Radioactive decay

Radioactive decay occurs when **unstable** atomic nuclei decay, by the emission of alpha particles, beta particles or gamma rays. Radioactive decay is **random** in nature – you cannot tell if any one particular atom will decay, but if you have a large number of the same atoms you can tell the proportion of atoms that will decay in a given time. As a result of this random nature, if we are going to do experiments involving the measurement of radioactive decay, we must take repeat readings over lengthy periods, and then average the results.

Penetrating power

Alpha (α), beta (β) and gamma (γ) radiation can be distinguished from each other by their penetrating power into different materials. Alpha radiation is the least penetrating and is stopped by a thin sheet of paper or a few centimetres of air. Beta radiation is stopped by a few millimetres of aluminium or Perspex, and gamma rays are the most penetrating, having the ability to pass through several centimetres of lead.

Gamma rays, being the most penetrating, generally pass straight through our bodies, causing little damage. Alpha radiation causes the most damage if it gets inside the body as it is absorbed easily by the cells in our bodies.

> **Examiner tip**
>
> It is important when you have questions that involve a choice of answers from a list that you read the choices very carefully. Sometimes the choices all seem valid, so you must read them carefully to find the correct answer.

Background radiation

Ionising radiation is naturally all around us. We are constantly surrounded by radioactive atoms that can decay emitting alpha, beta or gamma radiation. This can come from our food, buildings and the ground, in addition to the ionising radiation coming from space (collectively called cosmic rays).

There is also background radiation coming from human-made sources. Nuclear medicine, X-rays, nuclear power and reprocessing plants, and nuclear weapons explosions all contribute towards the total background radiation. Most of our total background radiation, though, comes from the rocks and soil around us. These contain uranium atoms that decay to eventually form radon gas, which is radioactive, and we breathe it in.

We measure the amount of radiation that we receive using the concept of **dose**. Dose is a measure of how much energy we receive from the ionising radiation – and it depends on the local background radiation. If we live in an area with large amounts of granite rock that contains high levels of uranium, we will receive a higher dose from the radon gas emitted by the rock.

If we are going to do experiments involving the measurement of radioactive decay we must take this background radiation into account. Before we do any experiments we must measure the local radioactive background count and then subtract this value from any counts that we subsequently make.

Nuclear waste

Revised

The waste materials produced by nuclear reactors will remain radioactive for a very long time. About 0.8 % of a used (or spent) fuel rod is uranium-235, which remains radioactive for millions of years. In fact, it takes about 703 800 000 years for a sample of uranium-235 to become half as radioactive. It takes about five times this value, about 3 500 000 000 years, before the radioactivity returns to a value similar to naturally occurring background radiation. This means that radioactive nuclear waste must be stored for a very long time inside very secure storage facilities with thick, lead-lined, concrete walls, to prevent alpha, beta and gamma radiation from escaping into the atmosphere. Underground storage may well be the only solution.

> **Examiner tip**
>
> Remember that with Quality of Written Communication questions like Question 28 part **c)**, the examiners will be looking for clear explanations. If you get the basic facts right but your explanation is not clear or lacks detail, you may lose marks. See pages 110–111 for more help answering QWC questions.

Check your understanding

Tested

28 Some radioactive elements emit more than one type of radiation. A Geiger counter was used to investigate the radiation emitted from a particular source which was placed close to the detector.

The table shows the average number of counts per minute when different absorbers were placed between the source and detector. All figures have been corrected for background radiation.

Original count/min with no absorber	Count/min with a paper absorber	Count/min with 3 mm aluminium absorber	Count/min with 1 cm lead absorber	Count/min with 2 cm lead absorber
1000	900	900	200	40

a) i) By how much does the 1 cm of lead change the original count rate? *(1 mark)*

ii) What type of radiation passes through 1 cm of lead? *(1 mark)*

b) i) State how much of the original count rate was produced by gamma radiation. *(1 mark)*

ii) Explain your answer. *(2 marks)*

c) The figures in this experiment are all 'corrected for background radiation'. State clearly what this means, explain why it is done, and include in your account what background radiation is and give its sources. *(6 marks QWC)*

Go online for answers

Online

The scale of the Universe

The Solar System

The Universe is a very big place – it would take about 13.75 thousand million (13.75 billion) years for light to travel from the Earth to the edge of the observable Universe!

Our local patch of the Universe is called the Solar System. The main constituents of the Solar System are:

- 1 star – the Sun
- 8 planets – Mercury, Venus, Earth, Mars, Jupiter, Saturn, Uranus and Neptune
- 146 moons (a moon is a natural satellite of a planet)
- 5 dwarf planets, including Pluto
- an asteroid belt – between Mars and Jupiter
- many comets and other small lumps of rock and interplanetary dust
- a surrounding 'halo' of rock, ice and dust called the Oort Cloud.

Patterns in the Solar System

The Solar System has many patterns and trends that can be deduced from data about the planets and moons. Many of these patterns relate to the energy released by the Sun and the distance of each planet from the Sun. The further away from the Sun, the colder the average surface temperature of a planet (with the exception of Venus which has a thick atmosphere and a huge greenhouse effect). The energy from the Sun spreads out as it gets further from the Sun. A distant planet therefore has less energy per square metre of area than a close planet.

The greater the distance of a planet from the Sun, the longer its year length. (The planet has to travel much further to make one orbit of the Sun.)

Measuring distances in the Universe

- **Earth radius**, R_e – the size of a planet is measured relative to the Earth, so the radius of Jupiter = 11 R_e. Comparisons to the Earth's dimensions are good measurements to use to compare the planets.

- **Astronomical Units**, **AU** – this is the average distance of the Earth from the Sun. Distances in the Solar System are measured using this unit. Neptune, the furthest planet, is 30 AU from the Sun and the Oort Cloud stretches out to over 100 000 AU! (1 AU = 1.5×10^{11} m.)

- **Light years**, **ly** – the light year is the distance that light travels in one year – 9.47×10^{15} m. This unit is used to measure distances to our nearest stars and within our own galaxy of stars, the Milky Way. The closest star to the Sun, Proxima Centauri, is 4.2 ly away. Our Solar System is about 4 ly in diameter, and the Milky Way is about 100 000 ly across!

> **Examiner tip**
>
> For Question **29** make sure that you study the diagram carefully – only two of the planets are shown. If you get a question like this in the exam you could sketch in the other planets on the exam paper.

Our galaxy is part of a 'Local Group' of galaxies, about 10 million ly across, and the Local Group is part of the Virgo Supercluster of galaxy clusters, about 110 million ly across. The Virgo Supercluster is one of the largest observed structures in the Universe. The edge of the observable Universe is 13 750 million ly away.

29 The diagram shows the orbits of Mars and Neptune around the Sun.

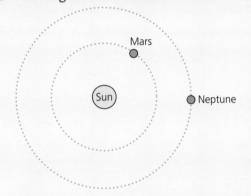

a) There are three planets between Mars and Neptune. Of these three:

  i)   name the planet closest to Mars. *(1 mark)*

  ii) name the planet closest to Neptune. *(1 mark)*

b) Neptune is bigger than Mars and further from the Sun. Give **two** other differences between Neptune and Mars. *(2 marks)*

30 The table gives data on six of the planets in the Solar System.

Planet	Distance from the Sun (million km)	Time for one orbit (years)	Length of day (hours)	Average surface temperature (°C)
Mercury	40	0.24	1420	197
Venus	110	0.62	5930	462
Earth	150	1.0	24	15
Mars	228	1.9	24.5	−23
Jupiter	778	11.9		−120
Saturn	1427	29.5	10.2	−180

a) Ceres is a dwarf planet. It orbits the Sun at a distance of 410 million km.

  i)   Suggest values for its orbit time and its surface temperature. *(1 mark)*

  ii) Explain your answers. *(2 marks)*

b) The table can be used to analyse patterns in the Solar System.

  i)   Plot a graph to show how the time a planet takes to orbit the Sun depends on the distance from the Sun, **for the first four planets only**. *(3 marks)*

  ii) Explain how the graph shows that the time for the orbit is not proportional to a planet's distance from the Sun. *(1 mark)*

  iii) Is there enough information in the **table** to estimate the length of a day on Jupiter? Give a reason for your answer. *(1 mark)*

Go online for answers ⸻⸻⸻⸻ Online ☐

Measuring the Universe and the Big Bang

Measuring the Universe

The first real measurements of the scale of the Universe were carried out using a technique called **stellar spectroscopy** by an astronomer called Edwin Hubble in 1929. Hubble knew that hot gases **absorbed** and **emitted** light with very **specific wavelengths** (and colours), uniquely characteristic of the elements making up the gas – like a fingerprint for each element!

During the nineteenth century, astronomers had discovered that they could use stellar spectroscopy to determine the composition of stars. The spectra of all stars contain black lines, where wavelengths have been removed from the continuous spectrum by elements that make up the star – this is called an absorption spectrum. By comparing these absorption spectra to the spectra of different elements here on Earth, astronomers can tell which elements are present in the star.

Hubble was the first person to use stellar spectroscopy to measure the speed of galaxies away from Earth using a phenomenon known as **redshift**. The absorption spectra of many stars appeared to be displaced or 'shifted' to slightly longer wavelengths (towards the red end of the spectrum, hence 'redshift') due to the stars in the galaxies moving away from the Earth.

Hubble's Law

Hubble surveyed many galaxies and plotted them against their distance away from Earth. He discovered that there was a relationship between the speed of the galaxy and its distance away from Earth, now known as Hubble's Law:

> 'The speed of recession is proportional to the distance of the galaxy away from Earth.'

> or 'The increase in redshift is proportional to the distance away from Earth.'

Hubble was also the first person to account for this pattern in 'cosmological' redshift. Hubble's theory was that the increase in redshift with distance was due to the expansion of the Universe that has occurred since the Big Bang – as the Universe expands, so the wavelength of the radiation is stretched!

The Big Bang

The Big Bang theory of the formation and subsequent evolution of the Universe was proposed as a way of explaining Hubble's measurements and his law. If the Universe began with a huge explosion, then it should still be expanding today. Cosmological redshift shows us that the rate of expansion is increasing; that is the expansion of the Universe is 'accelerating'.

The Big Bang theory also predicts that enormous amounts of energy, in the form of high energy gamma rays, would have been produced at the moment of the Big Bang. As the Universe expanded, stretching the fabric of space, so the wavelength of the gamma rays was stretched as well – the cosmological redshift. Over 13.75 billion years of expansion the wavelength has been stretched so much that the background remnant of these gamma rays now have the wavelength of microwaves – the Cosmic Microwave Background Radiation (CMBR), discovered by accident by Arno Penzias and Robert Wilson in 1964. They found that whatever direction they pointed their microwave telescope they always picked up the same background signal. They quickly realised that these signals were the remnant of the gamma rays produced at the moment of the Big Bang, cosmologically redshifted to microwave wavelengths!

Check your understanding

Tested

31 In 1842, the philosopher Auguste Comte commented that we could measure the distance and motion of planets and stars but we could never know anything about their composition. Twenty eight years earlier, the German scientist Fraunhofer had noticed dark lines in the spectrum of the Sun. Astronomers would later use these lines to prove the philosopher incorrect. The diagram shows (in grey) the spectrum of the Sun with these 'Fraunhofer lines' and a wavelength scale.

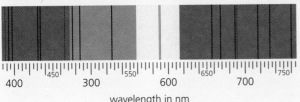

wavelength in nm

a) Explain how the Fraunhofer lines are formed and how they tell us about the composition of the Sun. *(2 marks)*

b) An astronomer observed the spectra of two newly discovered galaxies. It was seen that the lines in the spectra from both galaxies were 'redshifted' when compared with the spectrum of a laboratory light source. The diagram shows the same part of the spectrum from the three sources described above. What could the scientists deduce about the distance of these two galaxies from our own? Explain your answer. *(3 marks)*

spectrum from laboratory — violet ... red

spectrum from galaxy 1 — violet ... red

spectrum from galaxy 2 — violet ... red

32 The diagram shows dark lines seen on the visible spectrum of a star.

400 450 500 550 600 650 700
wavelength (nm)

a) Complete the table below. Identify the elements present in the star by putting a **Y** (yes) or **N** (no) in the last column of each row. *(1 mark)*

Element	Wavelengths (nm)	Present in the star?
Helium	447, 502	
Iron`	431, 467, 496, 527	
Hydrogen	410, 434, 486, 656	
Sodium	590	

b) Explain how and why these dark lines would appear in different positions in the spectrum of a star in a distant galaxy. *(2 marks)*

Go online for answers

Online

'Quality of Written Communication' questions

Every exam paper will have at least one 'Quality of Written Communication' question (higher-tier papers have two). They are always worth **6 marks**, and the marks are given for **how well you explain yourself** and for correct **spelling**, **grammar** and **punctuation**. In this guide, these questions always have 'QWC' next to the number of marks.

The mark scheme for each of these questions is basically the same, although obviously the science will vary. The appropriate science is called **indicative content** in the mark scheme. The indicative content is given in the mark scheme in bullet points, but you should **always** write your answers in extended prose.

Here is an example of a pupil's answer and how it would be marked.

Question

It has been suggested that waste plastics could be recycled and used to manufacture houses cheaply and quickly. Evaluate this potential use of waste plastics. *(6 marks QWC)*

In your answer you should refer to:

● the properties of plastics

● what happens to most plastics once they have been used

● the need to make the best possible use of the Earth's natural resources.

Mark scheme   Revised ☐

Indicative content:

This is the science that might be used in the answer, but not *all* of this has to be used. Remember, you need to write your answer in full sentences, not bullet points.

● Reference to the useful properties of plastics, for example resistance to corrosion and insulating properties. And to those properties which are not desirable in this case, for example flexibility and low density.

● Reference to the fact that most waste plastic is currently disposed of in landfill sites or burnt (incinerated) and the associated drawbacks.

● Reference to the benefits of re-using waste plastic, for example reduced amounts disposed of in landfill sites and that reserves of other resources, like timber and sand, are depleted less quickly or available for other uses.

5–6 marks	The candidate constructs an articulate, integrated account correctly linking relevant points, such as those in the indicative content, which shows sequential reasoning. The answer fully addresses the question with no irrelevant inclusions or significant omissions. The candidate uses appropriate scientific terminology and accurate spelling, punctuation and grammar.
3–4 marks	The candidate constructs an account correctly linking some relevant points, such as those in the indicative content, showing some reasoning. The answer addresses the question with some omissions. The candidate uses mainly appropriate scientific terminology and some accurate spelling, punctuation and grammar.
1–2 marks	The candidate makes some relevant points, such as those in the indicative content, showing limited reasoning. The answer addresses the question with significant omissions. The candidate uses limited scientific terminology and inaccuracies in spelling, punctuation and grammar.
0 marks	The candidate does not make any attempt or give a relevant answer worthy of credit.

Sample answer

Plastics have several properties that would be useful for making houses. They are strong and rigid and don't get rust or worn away by the weather. At the moment plastics are mostly disposed of in landfill sites or by being burnt, although they are being re-cycled more these days. Using waste plastics for houses is a type of re-cycling and this will help conserve natural resources and it will also help because it won't put so much pressure on landfill sites and stop them getting filled up so quickly.

Examiner's comment

The pupil's answer is **scientifically correct**, although some things have been left out – the properties of plastics that would not be suitable in houses and which 'natural resources' would be conserved. There are **no irrelevant comments**, and the points are linked together in a **logical sequence**. There is little use of **scientific terminology** ('rigid' is used, but the answer could have referred to 'corrosion' rather than 'rust', and could have used the term 'weathered'). There is a **grammatical error** ('get rust') and the last sentence is very long – it should have been broken into two or used commas. This counts as a **punctuation error**.

The answer seems to fit best within the 3–4 mark band and would be awarded **4 marks** because everything in the band has been achieved.

> ### Examiner tip
> With 'Quality of Written Communication' questions, remember:
> - Be careful with spelling, grammar and punctuation.
> - Try to put your ideas in a logical sequence, so that each idea follows on from the last one.
> - Use scientific terminology wherever you can.
> - Explain your ideas carefully, so that they are easily understood.
> - Write in full sentences and paragraphs; do not use bullet points.

The **Check your understanding** sections throughout this book give a lot of examples of the types of QWC questions that might be asked in an exam. Use them as practice and, if possible, get someone else to tell you if you've explained the ideas clearly (because it's difficult to judge your own writing).

Index